SAFe® to Scale

Scale

The practical guide to Scaled Agile for Product Managers and Product Owners

Valerio Zanini

SPC, CST, CPIT

SAFe® to Scale

Printed in the United States of America

ISBN (Paperback): 979-8-9903866-1-7

ISBN (Hardcover): 979-8-9903866-0-0

ISBN (E-Book): 979-8-9903866-2-4

We plant one tree for every copy of this book sold, in partnership with ForestPlanet.org

5D Vision Publishing, an imprint of 5D Vision, LLC

Printed in the U.S.A.

SAFe® to Scale

Foreword

Everything moves fast in the Digital Age. Customer desires, competitive threats, technology choices, business expectations, revenue opportunities, and workforce demands now happen at blistering speeds. This creates unprecedented challenges for organizations looking to harness this disruption for their benefit. By incorporating the power of Lean, Agile, and DevOps, SAFe helps organizations deliver innovative products and services faster. But speed is only one-half of the equation. Organizations that achieve Business Agility deliver truly innovative solutions that delight their customers. They exhibit a relentless focus on customer-centricity and product-first thinking.

Valerio Zanini's book, The Practical Guide to Scaled Agile for Product Managers and Product Owners, is a comprehensive handbook for Product Managers and Product Owners who play a crucial role in defining and delivering new products and solutions. It provides a solid foundation for learning about the critical aspects of the Framework with a deeper focus on applying product-based thinking in SAFe. Written from personal experience gained during multiple SAFe implementations, Valerio includes many case studies, examples, tips, and techniques, as well as advice from thought leaders across the Lean-Agile community, ensuring the book has direct practical application.

One key to product success is highlighted in SAFe Principle #1, Take an Economic View, which guides Product Leaders to make decisions in a proper economic context. In support of this principle, Valerio encourages all those in product roles to recognize the difference between optimizing 'outcomes' over 'outputs' and illustrates how iterative approaches using MVPs can reduce the risk inherent in product development. Valerio also cautions organizations from becoming simple Feature Factories where the goal of delivering more functionalities more quickly can become disconnected from the objective of maximizing customer value. He describes approaches to rectify this problem, including using a Product Journey Map that creates a unified view of the customer persona, the customer journey, and the potential new features.

Whether you are an experienced Product Manager or Product Owner wanting to deepen your knowledge or just beginning your journey and looking for guidance on how to be effective in your new role, this book will help. The value of SAFe always comes from its successful application, and this book provides the opportunity to learn directly from an experienced guide.

Stay SAFe.

Andrew Sales

Chief Methodologist, SAFe Fellow, and SPCT

Foreword

In an era defined by rapid technological advancement and digital transformation, the role of Product Managers and Product Owners has evolved significantly and become more critical. As enterprises navigate the complexities of the modern business landscape and strive to thrive with business agility, the Agile ways of working at scale have emerged as essential strategies for achieving business agility. Thus, adoption and adaptation of the Scaled Agile Framework (SAFe) have become paramount.

This book, SAFe® to Scale by Valerio Zanini, serves as a comprehensive guide for Product Managers and Product Owners seeking to scale agile ways of working within their unique contexts. By applying Agile values and principles to their enterprises, they can effectively harness the power of generative AI, Big Data, Cloud, and DevOps - elements that are both disruptive and enabling in nature.

Through a blend of practical insights, real-world examples, and expert advice from experienced SPCs and SPCTs, readers will gain a deep understanding of how to leverage these transformative technologies to drive innovation, collaboration, and adaptability. The journey to thriving in today's digital era requires a nuanced approach that embraces change, fosters creativity, and prioritizes continuous improvement.

As the digital era continues to unfold with the evolving role of Product Managers and Product Owners, the ability to adapt and thrive in the face of constant change is essential. This book serves as a beacon and a valuable resource for Product Managers and Product Owners seeking to embrace the challenges of today's dynamic business environment emerging as catalysts and leading their organizations towards sustainable success.

Embark on this journey of discovery and transformation with Valerio Zanini to unveil the secrets of unleashing business agility in the digital era, one SAFe agile step at a time.

Vikas Kapila

SAFe Practice Consultant-T (SPCT), Accredited Kanban Trainer

Foreword

In the world of Agile, where every company out there is on a rat race to get their teams Agile certified in anticipation of winning a golden egg with ease, most of them, if not all, fail to recognize the fact that it's not that straightforward. Just working in an Agile way is not enough to pull it through. What is critical here is to understand that a Product way of thinking and execution should take center stage. And that is the value-add from our dear friend Valerio - who is diligently focusing on changing the world through education and coaching with his product thinking knowledge.

Through his initial publications, Valerio provided the world with product related knowledge, and through this book, he provides us all with an excellent approach to plan and scale the execution of work in a typical organization. He did a meticulous job of blending the current scaling frameworks and associated events with product thinking, to help an organization come out in flying colors. It is an easy read with good context that can be applied to an organization with ease. For everything else, you can always reach out to him.

Finally, I must admit that this is a gem of a collection of things to help an organization with scaling up, and I would definitely recommend this to every agilist out there ... GOOD LUCK and ENJOY THE SUCCESS this book brings to your organization.

Ramesh Nori

SAFe Practice Consultant-T (SPCT)

Table of Contents

Introduction

Over the years, I have helped many organizations learn and adopt SAFe practices including McKesson, CMS Medicare, Dassault Systèmes, Capital One, and Wesco Distribution. I have learned a lot of lessons regarding what works well with SAFe, what is challenging, what is easy for teams to implement, and what is hard.

Many organizations struggle with adopting product practices that drive value for their customers and their own business. I believe that **a product thinking mindset is essential to a successful implementation of SAFe®**. If the product idea and its plan are not solid, even the best agile practices will not help the company build a better product.

The inspiration for this book came from observing one of these companies implement all the ceremonies of SAFe but struggle to properly empower its Product Managers and Product Owners to define a successful product. This book equips you with not only SAFe knowledge but also tips and real-life stories to help product teams adopt it effectively. It focuses on the work of Product Managers and Product Owners within the context of SAFe, but it can be useful for anyone who wishes to implement SAFe more effectively.

I do not cover all of the ins and outs of SAFe, nor do I replace the extensive learning that happens in a SAFe training and certification class. If you are curious and want to continue your learning journey, Scaled Agile offers numerous courses in SAFe and in certification programs. In fact, you can start exploring by visiting: www.scaledagile.com.

If you want to reach out for comments or questions, please connect with me via vzanini@5dvision.com or via www.linkedin.com/in/vzanini.

Introduction to SAFe®

The SAFe Framework

The Scaled Agile Framework® (SAFe®) is the world's leading framework[i] for scaling agile practices for dozens or for even hundreds of agile teams. It integrates the power of Lean, Agile, and DevOps into a comprehensive operating system that helps enterprises thrive in today's digital age by delivering innovative products and services faster, more predictably, and with better quality.

SAFe provides a structured approach to scaling agile practices across large and complex organizations. It helps enterprises do the following:

- Align teams around a common vision and shared goals.
- Improve communication and collaboration between teams.
- Reduce risk and uncertainty for complex projects.
- Accelerate time to reach the targeted market.
- Deliver value to customers more efficiently and more frequently.
- Increase business agility and respond to market changes more rapidly.

Because SAFe can help organizations of different sizes scale their agile implementations, it can be applied to just a few agile teams, or to hundreds of teams. SAFe adds its own roles, responsibilities, and artifacts. SAFe also provides a set of tools and resources to help organizations implement and to adopt the framework.

SAFe is based on 4 key values:

- **Alignment:** All teams and all stakeholders must be aligned around the organization's common vision and goals.
- **Visibility and Transparency:** Work and progress must be visible and transparent to everyone who is involved.
- **Respect for People:** We respect all of the people who perform the work as professionals.
- **Relentless Improvement:** Teams must continuously learn and improve their practices.

When these values are embodied by an organization, they create the foundation on which a scaled agile implementation can be built. Applying these values often requires a shift in how the company operates and in its culture.

SAFe is a framework – a set of practices, roles, and principles – that companies can apply to scale their product development teams. However, SAFe is not a silver bullet: just applying it blindly and following the "instructions manual," does not guarantee success. The key to a successful SAFe adoption lies in adapting the framework to the needs and to the reality of the organization, and in driving a mindset shift toward agility.

I believe that for SAFe (or for any agile implementation) to be successful, the critical path includes empowering the product people to make the right decisions on the product they are building.

This book provides an explanation of how SAFe works and offers tips to Product Managers and Product Owners on how to implement it effectively.

The Case for Scaling with SAFe

SAFe is maintained by Scaled Agile, Inc., which is based in Colorado. Scaled Agile launched SAFe in 2011 and has continuously updated the framework. As of this date, SAFe is now at version 6[ii].

According to Scaled Agile, over 20,000 companies worldwide use SAFe today[iii]. This includes some of the world's largest and most successful companies, such as Airbus, BMW, Cisco, GE, Intel, Lockheed Martin, and NASA.

SAFe is popular because it provides a comprehensive framework for scaling Agile practices across large and complex organizations. It helps organizations to improve alignment and communication, to reduce risk and uncertainty, and to accelerate time to market.

Here are some of the reasons why so many companies use SAFe today:

- It is a proven framework for scaling Agile practices across large and complex organizations.

- It is flexible and can be adapted to meet the specific needs of each organization.

- It is supported by a large and active community of practitioners.

- It can be adopted by a few Agile Teams in an ART, and then scaled to more teams or more ARTs, as needed.

- It is a steppingstone towards embracing business agility.

If you are working in a large and complex organization, then SAFe is a framework that you should consider. SAFe can help you to improve your organization's agility and to deliver value to customers more effectively.

There Can Be No True Agility Without Product Thinking

It is often said that if the teams are not adopting Scrum practices effectively, they will struggle with SAFe.

The same can be said about proper Product Management. If teams are not adopting the right product practices, they risk that what they build will not be valuable – for either the business or the customer. Yes, the organization may be adopting SAFe, they may be "running" the right events, they may be building stuff, but if Product Management does not properly focus, prioritize, and validate solutions – well, the end result may be a ton of waste.

While there are many reasons why Agile and SAFe transformations struggle to take off, the lack of proper product thinking is often a culprit. In fact, even the best Agile Teams **cannot deliver much value if proper product visioning, prioritization, and validation practices are not in place or properly followed**. Instead, Agile gets the blame and the teams become resistant to change.

I recently was asked to help a large team that was building a strategic digital platform that the company direly needed. The team was working hard, was putting in long hours, and was solving major problems. But the leadership kept changing the overall vision for this product, and with it, the priorities of what to build. For the team it was difficult to focus and to get anything completed before the next change. After months of development, they had nothing in production.

The problem was not with poorly adopted Agile practices. The problem was with poor product practices that did not support the application of important principles needed for Agile to flourish.

You may get away with poorly implemented Agile practices, but, if you do not have the right product practices, you may be wasting your investment or be doomed from the start.

A blind application of SAFe will not cure all illnesses. Even the most faithful agilist who diligently executes the practices, will have a hard time reaping the benefits and delivering value to customers, if the right mindset and culture is not in place. **A development team cannot do it alone. The organization must provide the culture, the vision, and the empowerment that is needed for success.**

Infusing an effective product thinking mindset is key to the success of a product initiative and to a SAFe Agile transformation. Therefore, I always spend as much time working with teams and with their leadership in adopting the right product practices as I spend on SAFe practices. I make sure that the organizations understand the importance and the value of having a customer-centric approach, and that they understand the customer needs and what benefits the new product would deliver to the end users.

The product team should spend the right amount of time in discovery mode, talking with stakeholders and end users, testing prototypes, and refining ideas. This is true not only at the beginning of the project, but, also throughout its development. Product plans should not be top-down imposed by leadership, but, iterated and refined by the very people who are responsible for delivering valuable solutions to the customers: the product team.

Understand what the market needs your product to do and what problems the customers have. Validate your hypotheses with real users, get feedback from them, and measure the outcomes. Instead of making a major upfront plan and using SAFe to build one increment at a time, map out the most critical features your customers need and validate the solution as quickly as possible. Learn what works and what does not, and then iterate on the plan with the next set of features.

There can be no true Agility without product thinking: This book equips product teams with the right product thinking mindset and practices, enabling them to build great products and achieve success with SAFe.

The Scaled Agile Framework® (SAFe®)

In this chapter we are going to look at the SAFe framework and how it helps to answer these questions:

"How do we scale from one team to many teams, and how do we maintain alignment between all of these teams?"

As we have seen before, the fundamental building blocks of SAFe are the Agile Teams. When we move from one team to several teams, that is where the complexity starts to show up. Because if we have multiple teams all working together on the same product, there will be, of course, dependencies, scheduling conflicts, and different priorities.

Every team may have different levels of competency or expertise.

"How do we bring everybody to the same level? How do we help teams sync up with each other on dependencies and timelines?"

These are examples of the challenges that multiple teams working together may face. This is what SAFe is designed to address.

The Four Levels in SAFe

Scaling from one Agile Team to tens or hundreds of Agile Teams, requires creating some structure around the teams, synchronizing the work, aligning on priorities, and managing dependencies.

SAFe does this with 4 levels:

Team Level: This is where the actual development work happens. The Team level is composed of the Agile Teams. Agile Teams typically use Scrum or Kanban, and work independently with their own set of priorities and objectives. They synchronize their development activities, integrate their increments into a larger product, and manage cross-team dependencies. SAFe organizes the teams into ARTs (Agile Release Trains).

ART Level: The ART is the first structure that SAFe creates. It is formed by putting together a group of Agile Teams that work on the same value stream. Typically, an ART includes 5 to 12 Agile Teams. Each ART plans its work in increments of 4 to 6 Sprints called the Planning Interval (PI) and the teams do this at PI Planning.

NOTE: The ART level was called Program level before SAFe 6.0 – I use these terms interchangeably throughout this book.

Large Solution Level: When the organization is building a very large solution that spans multiple value streams, or potentially more than 12 Teams, it needs multiple ARTs. The Large Solution level organizes multiple ARTs into a Solution Release Train, scaling up the ART structure. A Solution Release Train can span dozens of teams and includes additional roles to manage its complexity. When needed, a Solution Release Train also includes teams from external suppliers.

Portfolio Level: The Portfolio level is the fourth and highest level in SAFe. It is required when the organization needs to make budget, strategic, or priority decisions among large initiatives. These may represent different major functionalities to add to a product or may represent different products. To make trade-off decisions and to decide on which initiative to focus capacity and financial resources, these initiatives are managed as a portfolio. SAFe introduces additional roles and elements in the framework to properly manage the portfolio.

	Backlog Category	Backlog Owner	Technical Owner	Agile Coach
PORTFOLIO	Portfolio Backlog	Lean Portfolio Management / Epic Owner	Enterprise Architect	Lean Agile Center of Excellence
SOLUTION	Solution Backlog	Solution Manager	Solution Architect	Solution Train Engineer
ART	ART Backlog	Product Management	System Architect	Release Train Engineer
TEAM	Team Backlog	Product Owner	Team Members / Developers	Scrum Master / Team Coach

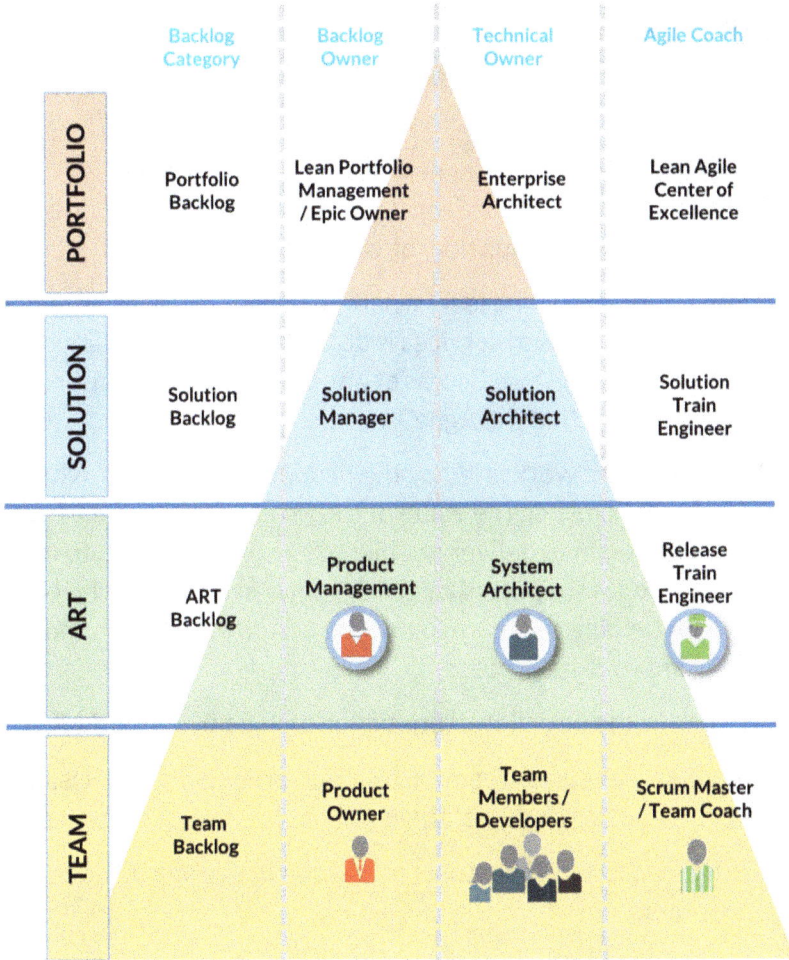

This is an overview of the SAFe framework's structure. Not all levels may be present in all organizations: some organizations only need an ART level to manage the work between maybe 10 teams; some organizations need to manage a large number of teams, including external suppliers, or multiple value streams, and they implement the Large Solution level; other organizations need to add a Portfolio level to manage work across a portfolio of initiatives.

SAFe offers a flexible approach to scale Agile and to fit the needs of different organizations of different sizes[iv]. In the next few sections, I will provide additional details about each of the 4 levels, starting with the Team level:

Team Level

We said earlier that the fundamental team structure in SAFe is the Agile Team which exists at the Team level. Agile Teams enable the Team Flow to be a continuous flow of value to customers.

The Team level in SAFe is the level where the actual work of developing and delivering products and services is done. It is the foundation of SAFe and is essential for the success of any SAFe implementation. This is the level where you find the Agile Teams.

At the Team level, the work is led by the Product Owner (PO), who is responsible for maximizing the value of the Product Backlog and for working with the team to deliver the highest priority features to customers. The PO is supported by the Scrum Master (SM), who is responsible for helping the team follow the Scrum framework and continuously improve its process.

Here are some of the key characteristics of the Team level in SAFe:

- Empowered teams: Teams are empowered to make decisions and to take ownership of their work.

- Customer focus: Teams are focused on delivering value to customers.

- Continuous improvement: Teams are continuously improving their process and delivering better products and services to customers.

The Team level is an essential part of SAFe and it is the first building block for any organization that is looking to improve its agility and to deliver value to customers more effectively. I believe that it is also the most important level: if the teams are not adopting the right practices or do not employ an agile mindset, they will struggle to deliver valuable products, and any efforts in scaling SAFe across the rest of the organization will suffer. In a later chapter, we will talk more about Agile Teams.

ART Level

When you scale up from one Agile Team to multiple Agile Teams working together, SAFe introduces a new structure called the Agile Release Train. At this level, we have an ART Backlog managed by Product Management, and we have a System Architect who oversees the overall architecture. We also have the Release Train Engineer (RTE) who oversees the coaching and alignment between all of the different teams in collaboration with the Scrum Masters.

The ART level in SAFe is the level that coordinates the work of multiple Agile Teams to deliver a common value stream. It is the cornerstone of SAFe and is essential for scaling Agile practices across large and complex organizations.

The ART level is coordinated by the Release Train Engineer, who is responsible for facilitating communication and collaboration between the teams, managing risks and dependencies, and ensuring that the ART is on track to meet its goals. The RTE is supported by the Scrum Masters and by other key stakeholders.

Here are some of the key benefits of using the ART level in SAFe:

- Improved alignment and coordination between teams
- Reduced risk and uncertainty
- Accelerated time to market
- Improved quality of the products and services delivered
- Increased customer satisfaction
- Alignment on schedules and deliverables among multiple teams

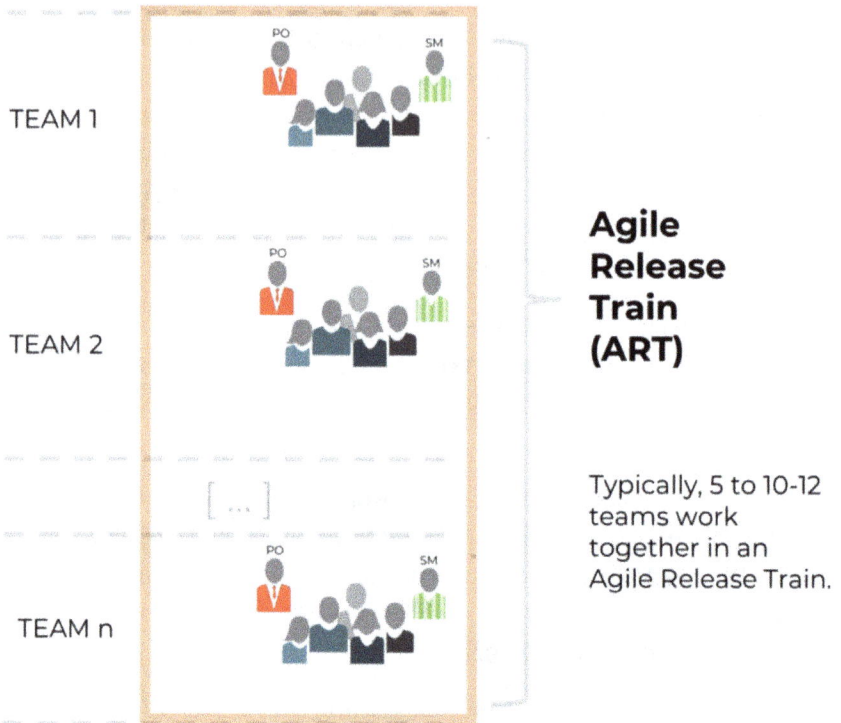

TEAM 1

TEAM 2

[...]

TEAM n

Agile Release Train (ART)

Typically, 5 to 10-12 teams work together in an Agile Release Train.

These activities are typically performed at the ART level in SAFe:

PI Planning: PI Planning is typically a 2-day event where the teams and stakeholders come together to plan the upcoming Planning Interval. This includes identifying the work that needs to be done, estimating the effort required, and assigning the work to the teams.

Inspect and Adapt: Inspect and Adapt is an event held at the end of the PI where the teams come together to review their performance, to identify any challenges, and to identify opportunities for improvement. This is like a retrospective for the entire ART.

System Demo: The System Demo is a biweekly event where the teams integrate the work into a larger increment, and then demonstrate the integrated work to the stakeholders and to the customers. This is an opportunity to get feedback on the product and to identify any areas for improvement.

PO Sync: PO Sync is typically a weekly meeting between Product Management and the POs in an ART to discuss progress, to align on priorities, and to solve impediments.

Coach Sync: This is typically a weekly meeting between the RTE and the Scrum Masters in an ART to align on progress, to discuss impediments, and to identify opportunities to help the teams improve their performance. Sometimes called Scrum of Scrums or S2.

"The ART structure can scale up when we have 10 or 12 teams, but what if we have hundreds of teams working together on the same product?"

The ART becomes too big and unmanageable. That is when we introduce the Large Solution.

Large Solution Level

SAFe supports an additional level, called the Large Solution level. This level helps the organization to further scale beyond the first 10-12 teams in one ART. The Solution Release Train is composed of several Agile Release Trains (which can be augmented with external suppliers, if needed).

At the Large Solution level, we have a Solution Backlog which contains larger work items (called Capabilities) that then get split into smaller items in the ART Backlogs belonging to each train.

Also, at the Large Solution level we have new SAFe roles. We have Solution Management that manages the Solution Backlog. We have a Solution Architect who oversees the overall solution architecture. And we have a Solution Train Engineer who works with the different Release Train Engineers to sync up and to align the coaching and the support for all of the teams.

Notice how the Large Solution level replicates the structure of the ART level while scaling up to hundreds of teams.

The Large Solution level is responsible for the following:

- Defining the solution's vision, intent, and backlog

- Aligning the ARTs and external suppliers around the solution goals

- Coordinating the development and delivery of the solution

- Managing risks and dependencies across multiple ARTs

- Measuring and reporting on progress

The Large Solution level is coordinated by the Solution Train Engineer for alignment among the ARTs.

The Large Solution level is essential for the successful delivery of large, complex solutions. By providing coordination and alignment, the Large Solution level helps to reduce risk, to improve quality, and to accelerate time to market.

Portfolio Level

A Portfolio level is typically useful when we have an organization that is working on multiple products and needs to allocate resources and budgets across the different products in the portfolio.

An example is Microsoft: the company has a portfolio of products such as Microsoft Office, Windows, Azure, and Xbox 360. It even owns several video game companies and a search engine (Bing).

At the organizational level, we often need to make trade-off decisions between the different products in the portfolio for budgeting reasons, or for strategic reasons. On which parts of our portfolio are we going to focus more? For example, in the case of Microsoft, a portfolio decision may prioritize the work on the next release of Microsoft Windows versus work on Azure or on Xbox 360.

And so, decisions made at the Portfolio level will drill down to the Solution level, then to the different Agile Release Trains, and ultimately to the Agile Teams to get executed.

The Portfolio level is coordinated by the Lean Portfolio Management (LPM), who is responsible for implementing and for maintaining a Lean-Agile governance model. This model helps to ensure that the organization's investments are aligned with its strategic goals and that the Portfolio is delivering value to customers.

At the Portfolio level, we have a Portfolio Backlog. This backlog contains major product initiatives that we call Epics. In SAFe, the Epic Owner shepherds the Epics through the different stages in the Portfolio Kanban. We have an Enterprise Architect who oversees the architecture at the Enterprise level. And we have a Lean-Agile Center of Excellence, which is a group of people who oversee the agile implementation or the agile transformation within the organization. They work together with the Solution Train Engineers, the Release Train Engineers, and the Scrum Masters to guide the teams in doing their work.

These are some examples of the activities that are typically performed at the Portfolio level in SAFe:

Portfolio Kanban: The Portfolio Kanban is a lean-agile approach to portfolio management that helps to visualize and to optimize the flow of work across the portfolio.

Portfolio Backlog: The Portfolio Backlog is a prioritized list of all of the Epics that the organization needs to deliver in order to achieve its strategic goals.

Lean Budget: The Lean Budget is a flexible and responsive budget allocation that allows the organization to allocate resources to the most important work at any given time.

By using the Portfolio level, you can improve alignment between strategy and execution, reduce risk and uncertainty, and increase portfolio performance.

Additional Roles Introduced by SAFe

When we scale from one team to many Agile Teams working together, SAFe determines additional roles. These roles are at the ART level or above, and are required to create alignment and focus among all of the Agile Teams.

In the following sections I will focus on the roles needed to support an Agile Release Train at the ART level.

Agile Release Train (ART)

The fundamental structure in SAFe is a group of Agile Teams that we call an Agile Release Train. Typically, an ART includes 5 to 10 or maybe 12 teams and they are all working together on building a larger product.

An Agile Team starts its work with a Team Backlog based on priorities, then it executes the work one iteration (one Sprint) at a time. At the end of the Sprint, the team has produced an increment, which is the end result of its work for that Sprint or iteration.

When you have only one team working on its own, at the end of the Sprint the team does the Sprint Review to present the increment to the stakeholders and to the customers, and gets feedback.

When you have multiple teams working together, the Sprint Review typically takes a slightly different format because we have the scale. The teams put all of the increments together, producing a larger increment. And then, the teams present this product increment to the stakeholders and to the customers at what is typically called a System Demo. It is a similar thing as a Sprint Review; it is just that we do it at scale with all of the teams participating with the stakeholders and customers looking at the overall product increment built together by the different teams.

Each Sprint, the ART integrates the Increments produced by all teams into the larger Product Increment for the entire ART.

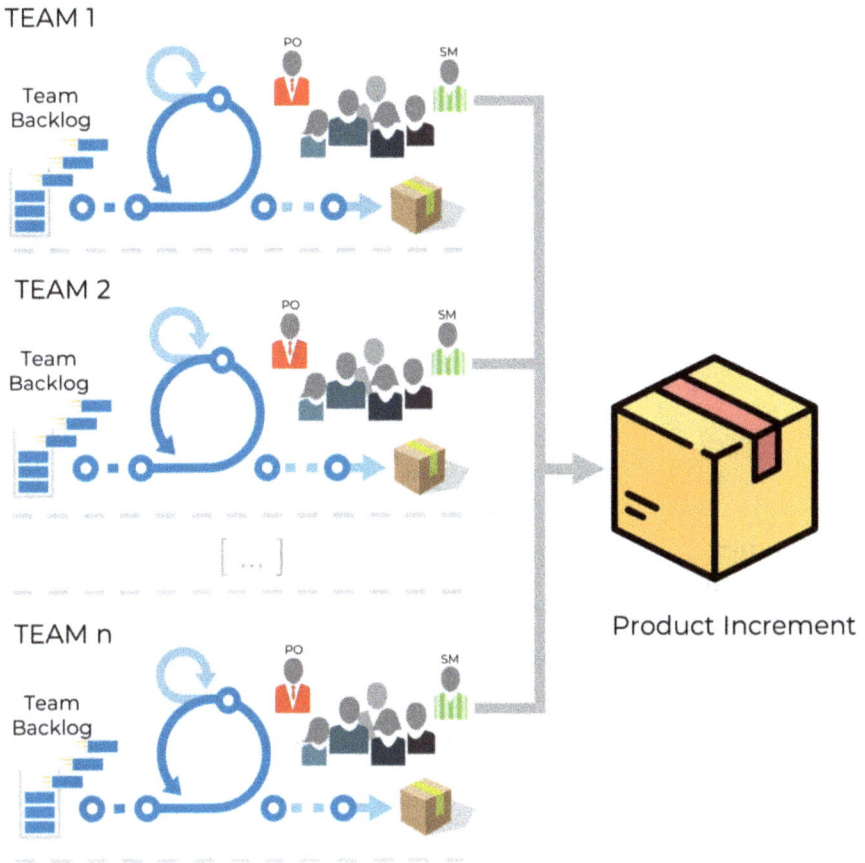

Product Increment

Product Management / Product Manager

Another change in SAFe is the concept of scaling the role of the Product Owner. When we have multiple teams, every team has its own Product Owner.

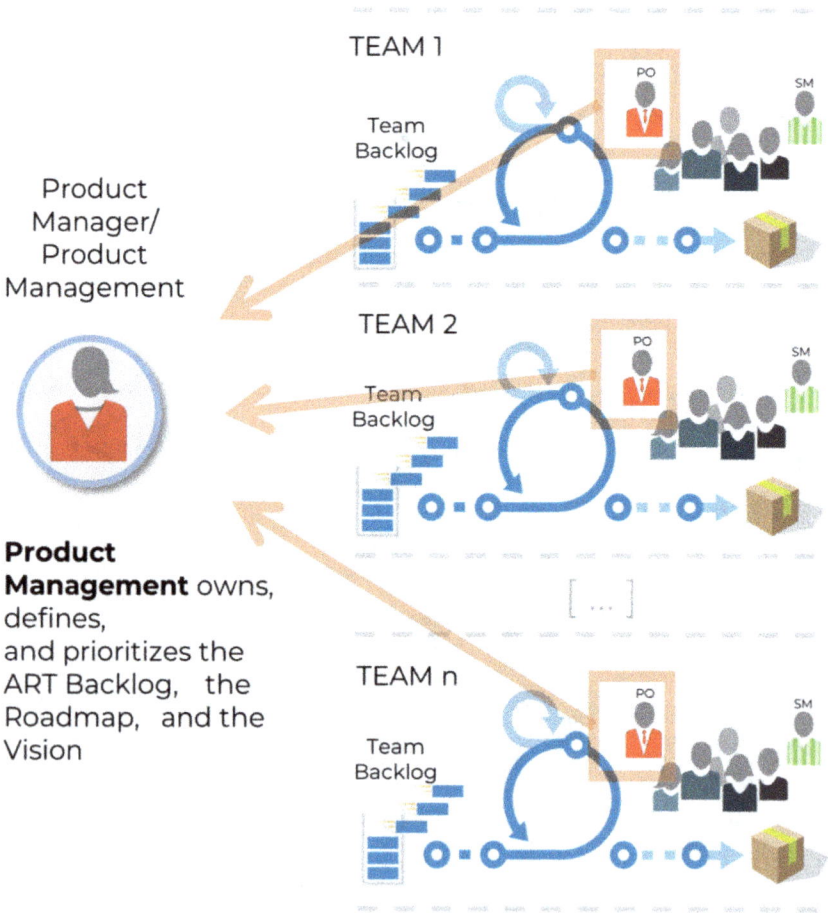

Product Manager/ Product Management

Product Management owns, defines, and prioritizes the ART Backlog, the Roadmap, and the Vision

"But how do we keep the work aligned? How do we keep the priorities aligned? Who provides a higher-level view of the priorities and of the overall vision for the product?"

In SAFe, there is an additional role called Product Management. Product Management is a function, not necessarily a person. Often, this role is covered by a Product Manager, but in complex product organizations, the role can be covered by a product team.

Starting in SAFe 6.0^v, we call it Product Management instead of Product Manager to highlight the fact that the role may be covered by a team of product people for large or complex products.

The Product Manager is like a Product Owner, but they work at a higher level. And the Product Manager owns, defines, and prioritizes what is called the ART Backlog (in versions prior to SAFe 6.0 this was named the Program Backlog, with the same meaning).

The ART Backlog is a higher-level list of the work and the priorities that the entire ART needs to do. The Product Manager also owns the product vision and the roadmap for their product.

The Product Owners from the Agile Teams and the Product Manager, of course, need to sync up their work, and to get aligned on all of the priorities that they need to do. The Product Manager manages the ART Backlog and identifies high-level priorities in the ART Backlog. Then, these high-level priorities get broken down and distributed to the individual Team Backlogs so that the Product Owners can prioritize the work in their Team Backlogs, and then execute the work with the Agile Teams.

SAFe Has Multiple Product Ownership/Management Layers

By Yuval Yeret, SPCT

As organizations tackle bigger products, they have some alternatives for how to tackle product ownership/management. Scrum advises having one Product Owner for each Product, even if multiple teams develop the Product. This is at the core of scaling frameworks such as Nexus and LeSS. SAFe takes a path that is more aligned with the classic structure of Product Management organizations which is to have multiple layers of Product ownership/management.

Product Owners own product at the Agile Team level. Product Managers own product at the team of teams level (Agile Release Train). Solution Managers own product for huge teams of teams working on even larger products/solutions.

Why did SAFe make this choice?

SAFe takes the perspective of learning from experience in the trenches and what patterns organizations are using and applying lean/agile principles as needed to help organizations evolve.

The advantage of this approach is that it aligns with the Product Manager/Owner journey. Working closely with one or two teams, owning product choices for a couple of product features or a certain slice of the product can be a great jumping point for Junior Product Managers/Owners.

As the Product Manager/Owner gains experience, they can take on a whole product themselves. It takes time for a Product Owner/Manager to gain the experience to act as the visionary entrepreneur for their product. They might start feeling more comfortable writing stories and executing experiments and, over time, learn to influence, design product experiments, and make tougher prioritization decisions with multiple demanding stakeholders. In other words, Product Managers/Owners naturally evolve from focusing on tactics to strategy over time.

What are some downsides to splitting Product responsibilities between the Product Owner and Product Manager?

An anti-pattern we often see is that the PM/PO split allows an organization to staff the PO role with "story writers" and "project managers" – people who aren't empowered as Product Owners, and that reinforce the project mindset of requirement order-taking and managing scope-budget-timeline. This lack of empowerment leads to delays and an environment where the team is focused on outputs rather than outcomes.

Empowering Product Owners and their teams is a common challenge in SAFe and Scrum. What I've seen work well is carving out an appropriate product scope within which the Product Owner and team are empowered to figure out what to build to achieve the desired outcomes and optimize the value of that product or that aspect of a bigger product.

Doing this requires figuring out the product architecture and moving towards an empowering leadership style.

As in many other areas, SAFe takes the evolutionary approach. If you're a purist or a revolutionary, you'll probably struggle with it. Real-world practitioners are more likely to relate to the evolutionary approach. It's important to ensure that the PO/PM separation is not seen as an excuse to continue doing everything the same.

Product Managers and Product Owners – A Collaborative Relationship

Leaders implementing the PO/PM split should ensure healthy collaboration, involvement, and partnership across the product ownership/management team.

Product Managers should internalize the SAFe principles of unleashing the intrinsic motivation of knowledge workers, in this case, Product Owners. Product Managers have a role as lean/agile leaders to nurture the competence, awareness, and alignment in the product team that would enable them to decentralize control and let Product Owners own a certain slice of the product.

Product Managers and Product Owners should have conversations about what decisions make sense to centralize and which should be decentralized. And the goal of Product Managers should be to grow Product Owners over time so they can make more and more decisions – and minimize the decisions that need to be made centrally. This is key to scaling without slowing down decision-making while still maintaining and ideally improving outcomes in alignment with strategic goals.

Release Train Engineer (RTE)

A similar structure exists for the Scrum Masters. The role of the Scrum Master exists to help the team improve. But, when we have multiple teams working together, all of the Scrum Masters need to sync up and to align their activities to help all of the teams move forward and to improve their performance.

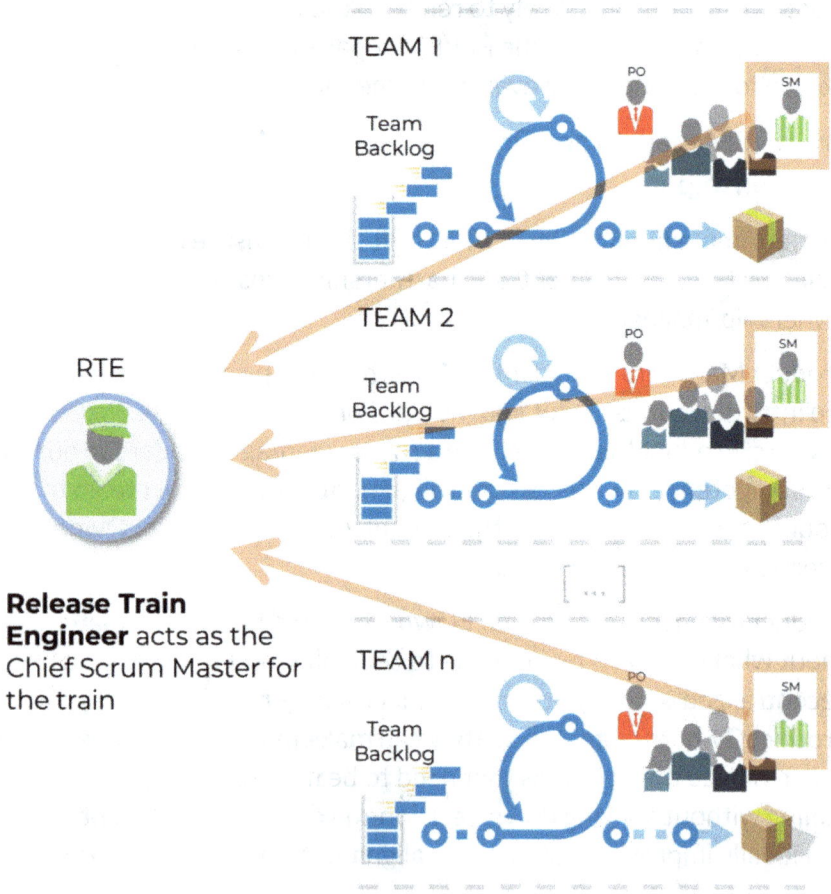

Release Train Engineer acts as the Chief Scrum Master for the train

To do that, we need a higher-level Scrum Master who oversees the SAFe adoption across all of the teams, and we call this person, the Release Train Engineer (RTE). You can think of it as the chief Scrum Master for the entire train.

The Scrum Masters and the RTE work together so that they can align their activities, share impediments, and share best practices on how to help their teams improve. The RTE also serves as a senior coach to the Scrum Masters, and in some organizations, the RTE is called the Scaled Scrum Master or the Agile Coach.

System Architect / Engineering

So far, we have covered how we scale the role of the Product Owner and the role of the Scrum Master. When we have multiple teams, there is one additional role that we need to look at and that is on the technical side.

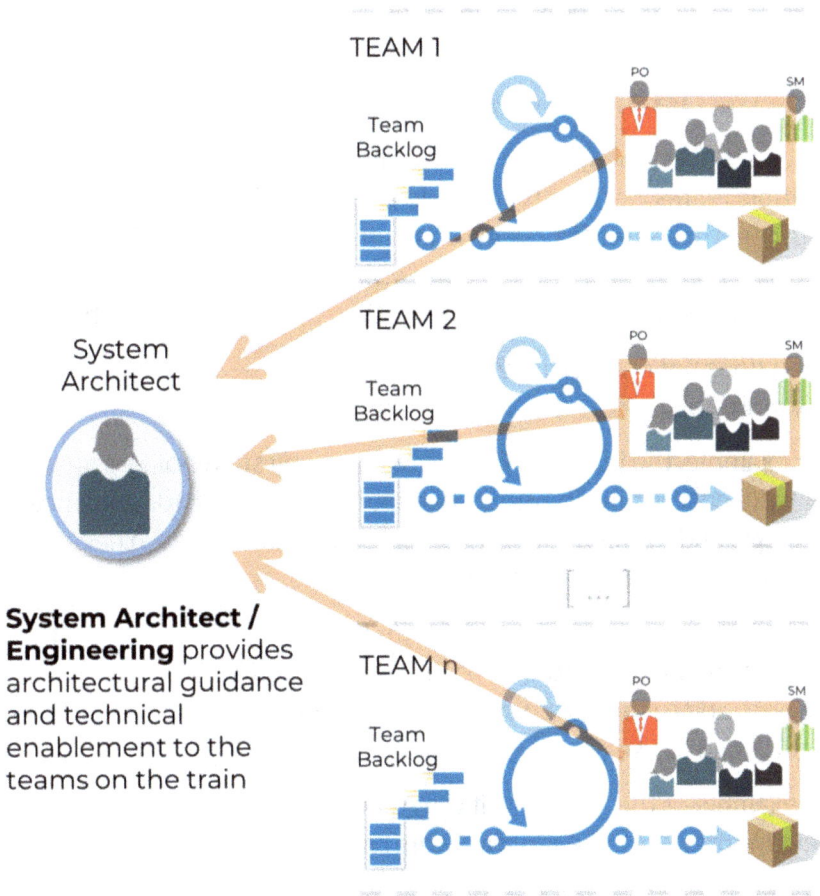

System Architect / Engineering provides architectural guidance and technical enablement to the teams on the train

"So, how do we scale the architecture and maintain alignment between multiple teams?"

There must be some level of alignment between the different team members on the different teams, so that they work well together.

In SAFe we have a higher-level role and that is the System Architect. The System Architect (sometimes called System Engineering) has the responsibility for providing architectural guidance to everybody on the train. It could be technical guidance, architectural guidance, enablement, and other types of responsibilities. So, the Team Members regularly sync up with the System Architect and with each other to identify technical dependencies and to align on the overall architecture.

Additional SAFe Roles

So, to put everything in one place, when we go from one team to multiple teams working together in an Agile Release Train, we need additional roles like Product Management scaling up the Product Owners, the Release Train Engineer scaling up the Scrum Masters, and the System Architect/Engineering scaling up the Team Members.

But it does not end here! Typically, on a SAFe release train, there are a few more roles.

For example, the Business Owners are the key stakeholders on the Agile Release Train. They provide input for priorities, for guidance on strategy, and for feedback on the increment that the train has presented at the System Demo.

Often, there is also the System Team. This is an additional team that works horizontally across all of the Agile Teams providing technical support, and for access to systems or to tools that all of the different teams need to use.

An example of this would be if the Agile Teams want to start adopting DevOps practices, the System Team can help each team to stand up a CI/CD (Continuous Integration/Continuous Deployment) pipeline, regression testing capabilities, and so on, to really enable DevOps practices across the train.

What Makes the RTE Job Interesting for You? What Makes It Challenging?

By Ajiri Ideh, RTE, SPC

The role of an RTE gives you a vantage position that I really like. I am able to visualize and impact the end-to-end flow of work. From working with Product Management, the Architects, Scrum Masters, and the entire delivery team, I am able to coach and support everyone.

This on the flip side could also be one of the challenges of the role, because you have quite a lot of internal and external stakeholders to juggle. While an RTE supports the team by providing training, coaching, etc., what I personally find as my most significant impact, is helping the train stay on track, as my vantage position enables me to forecast, plan, and preempt possible roadblocks.

Additional SAFe Events

SAFe adds a few events at the ART level (and above) to help teams plan their work together, to maintain alignment, and to manage dependencies. These events help establishing a closed-loop system with two interconnected cycles that drive continuous improvement and learning: at the Agile Team level, the cycle is represented by the Sprint; at the ART level, the cycle is represented by the PI (Planning Interval).

- Information from the inner loop (Sprints) feeds into the outer loop (PI). This allows the ART to adjust its plans based on real-time performance and feedback from the teams.

- Conversely, decisions made in the outer loop (PI) impact the inner loop (Sprints). For example, adjusted PI objectives may require changes to team backlogs and plans.

Planning Interval (PI) and PI Planning

If you have heard of SAFe before, chances are, you heard of PI Planning. This is probably the most famous SAFe construct, and we will dedicate a good portion of this book to it. PI Planning allows teams to really come together, to align their plans, and to identify dependencies.

Planning Interval (PI)

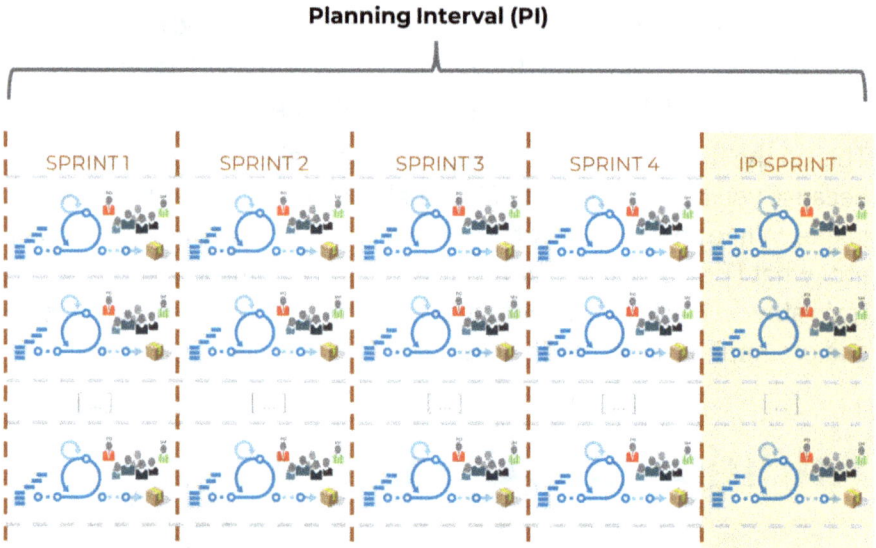

A Planning Interval (PI) is a set of Sprints, typically between 4 to 6 Sprints (including the IP Sprint). There is no fixed rule for how many Sprints are in a PI. Organizations may therefore match their planning cadence.

In SAFe, we define a Planning Interval as a group of Sprints, typically, 4 to 6 Sprints. A Planning Interval determines the rhythm for all of the Agile Teams on an ART that follow the same Sprint cadence for alignment, for planning, and for management of dependencies.

At the beginning of a new Planning Interval, we use PI Planning to plan the work that all of the teams are going to execute in that Planning Interval. So, PI Planning is a large event that we all do together. If you have 10 teams working together in an ART, all 10 teams participate in PI Planning.

At PI Planning, the teams look ahead at the next 4 to 6 Sprints, and then decide,

"What is it that we are going to focus on? What is it that we are going to execute and work on over the next few Sprints?"

Then, they create a plan together, identify dependencies, identify priorities, and determine the overall objectives for the PI.

Each PI focuses on achieving specific objectives. So, during PI Planning, each team identifies their own objectives:

"What are the goals that we would like to achieve by the end of the PI? What are the outcomes that we would like to deliver to our customers or to our stakeholders by the end of the PI?"

After each team has identified its list of objectives for the PI, we consolidate all of the objectives across the Agile Release Train into one set of objectives for the ART. These are the PI Objectives, and we will discuss them in an upcoming section.

Fast forward to the end of the PI... Once the 4 to 6 Sprints of the PI are completed, the Agile Teams meet again for another PI Planning session and there they plan the next set of Sprints (the next PI), and so on.

PO Sync

In order for the Product Owners and the Product Managers to successfully work together, they need to talk to each other, and they need to sync up. So, they organize what is called a PO Sync.

A PO Sync is a meeting between Product Management and all of the POs in the same ART, and the goals of this meeting are as follows:

- Align on priorities.
- Refine the ART Backlog into Team Backlogs.
- Track and share progress on the work and on PI Objectives.
- Resolve any impediments.
- Align on Vision, Roadmap, and overall objectives.

The PO Sync is a key meeting that typically happens once per week. So, every week, the Product Managers and the Product Owners sync up, align, and decide what to do next.

PO Sync

Product Owners and Product Management meet regularly (typically once per week) to:

- Align on priorities
- Refine the ART Backlog and align Team Backlogs
- Share progress on the work
- Resolve impediments
- Align on Vision, Roadmap, Objectives

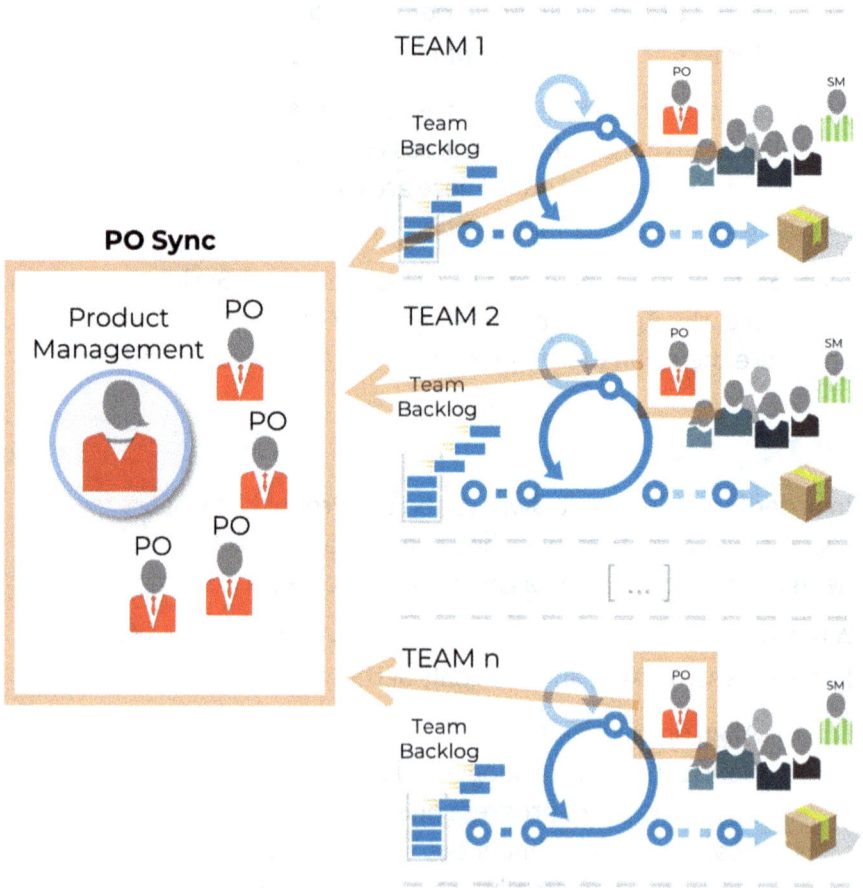

Coach Sync

To help the Scrum Masters and the RTE work together and sync up on the progress of each Agile Team, they typically organize a weekly meeting between the RTE and all of the Scrum Masters on the train. This meeting is also called Scrum of Scrum or S2.

Coach Sync /
Scrum of Scrum (S2)

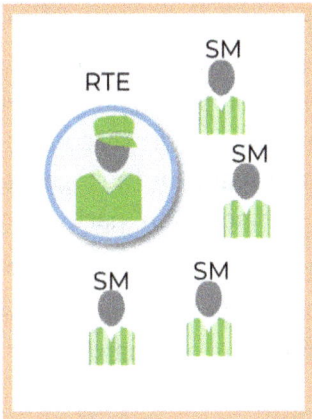

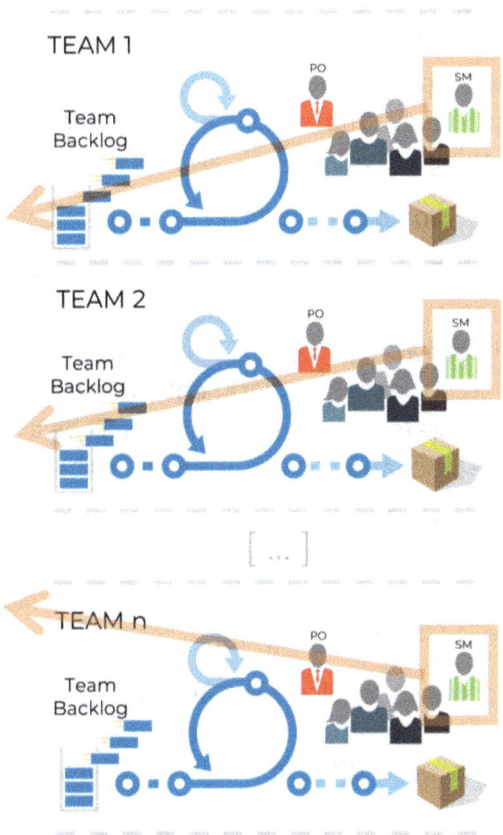

Scrum Masters and RTE meet regularly (typically once per week) to:

- Identify opportunities for team improvement
- Review and resolve impediments
- Align on activities to help the organization support the ART and adopt Agile/SAFe better

At the Coach Sync, they meet and discuss a variety of topics, including:

- Identifying opportunities for team improvement
- Evaluating the progress of the work performed by the Agile Teams to see if there are ways to help the teams improve
- Reviewing and resolving impediments
- Aligning activities to help the rest of the organization support the ART and adopt Agile and SAFe practices better

The teams in the ART can only be successful if the organization supports them by providing the right level of support, guidance, resources, access to stakeholders and customers, and visibility into priorities. Therefore, the RTE and the Scrum Masters also coach the rest of the organization in supporting the train.

IP Sprint

The IP Sprint (Innovation and Planning Sprint) is a dedicated Sprint left unplanned at the end of a PI to provide space for innovation and for planning activities. Typically, it is the last Sprint of a PI.

"Why should a team do an IP Sprint?"

The IP Sprint serves a couple of purposes. First, it gives the teams a little bit of space to learn new things, maybe a new type of technology, or to run a hackathon, or to implement a new development platform. It creates a space to experiment with new ideas that potentially could be incorporated into the product. It can be a useful space for the teams to drive innovation on the product. So that is the "innovation" part.

Then there is the "planning" part and that is basically when the next PI Planning event happens. The 2 or 3 days required for PI Planning take place within the IP Sprint. The Inspect & Adapt event also happens in the middle of the IP Sprint.

To enhance predictability and quality of the work, teams need to build "slack in the system." This can be achieved by not loading every developer to 100% utilization as well as having the IP Sprint as an "overflow" buffer.

What Shall We Do with the IP Sprint?

Some organizations struggle with the concept of an IP Sprint. They see it as a waste of time, and a detriment to the productivity of the teams. Having a Sprint every 4 to 6 Sprints that is not used for building new valuable features, is often met with resistance. When you do some math, the IP Sprint consumes between 16.7% and 25% of the capacity of the teams.

"So why do it?"

I have discussed the value of the IP Sprint in creating a space for innovation to happen. When teams are constantly under pressure to deliver new functionality, Sprint after Sprint, what they often miss is the time to stop, to reflect, and to learn new things. This is needed for innovation. The IP Sprint allows for it.

It also acts as a safeguard to deliver all of the work committed in the PI. During the PI, the teams work for several Sprints, building the product. And having that extra IP Sprint that is not filled with work, gives the teams a little bit of a breather to correct what is not working or to finish the work they had planned for the PI: it acts as a commitment buffer so that the teams are able to complete all of the work.

The IP Sprint Is Not for Hardening

A word of caution. In order to reap the benefits of the IP Sprint, the teams should not count on it to complete their work. The plan that they create at PI Planning should be a reasonable plan that they are able to execute and to deliver fully within the PI, excluding the IP Sprint.

The IP Sprint is not a "hardening Sprint" and is not a "stretch goal Sprint." The expectation is that whatever the teams plan for the PI, they are able to deliver it fully within the PI using the working Sprints (and not the IP Sprint).

The IP Sprint should be left alone to create that space for discovery, for innovation, and for technical spikes that create opportunities for the teams to grow. If, once in a while, it happens that some work extends into the IP Sprint, well that is life. We will deal with it. But we should not count on it.

Managing the IP Sprint

One of the reasons why the PI Sprints fail, is the lack of communication and follow-up. Instead, help the rest of the organization see the outcomes of the IP Sprint and consider it a useful investment of time, by doing the following:

- **Start with innovation:** Dedicate time for brainstorming, for ideation, and for exploring new possibilities. Use techniques like mind-mapping, rapid phototyping, and collaborative workshops to encourage creativity. Run a hackathon or a Design Sprint to validate some ideas with possible customers.

- **Practice new technologies:** Dedicate some time to play with new technologies. This will help the team members learn new things and possibly identify new opportunities for growing your product.

- **Refine and prioritize an innovation backlog:** Maintain an innovation backlog with possible ideas, new technologies to investigate, tools to implement that will help the team improve, and so forth. Evaluate the ideas based on feasibility, impact, and alignment with the overall goals. Decide with team members, which items from the innovation backlog to work on during the IP Sprint.

- **Focus on communication and collaboration:** Hold regular meetings, share updates, and encourage open discussion throughout the Sprint. Document the outcomes generated during the IP Sprint, what you accomplished, and what you learned from it. Share this document with all participants and stakeholders for reference.

- **Adapt to your specific context:** Tailor the approach based on your team size, project complexity, and organizational culture.

The Agile Team in SAFe

The Agile Team

Agile Teams represent the beating heart of SAFe. That is where the work takes place. The Agile Teams plan their work, influence the release plan, and build the product. Any SAFe implementation starts with organizing the Agile Teams and making sure that they work properly.

Agile Team

Agile Teams are cross-functional, self-organizing entities that can define, build, test, and deliver increments of value every Sprint.

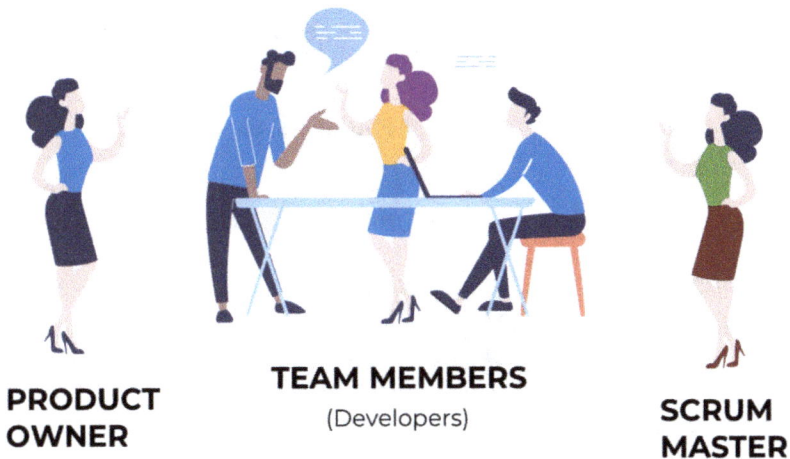

PRODUCT OWNER

TEAM MEMBERS
(Developers)

SCRUM MASTER

Typically, Agile Teams adopt Scrum, but SAFe can also incorporate teams that adopt Kanban. The two frameworks can coexist in SAFe.

Because most of the Agile Teams typically use Scrum, I will focus on this framework in this section.

"What is an Agile Team?"

It is a cross-functional group of people who are self-organizing, and who can define, build, test, and deliver an increment of value for every Sprint. It means that at the beginning of a Sprint, they decide what work they are going to do in the Sprint, basically, which User Stories they are going to select for the Sprint Backlog. And then, by the end of the Sprint, they self-organize in order to get the work done.

There are some specific responsibilities on the team. It's important to remember that these are accountabilities, not roles. This means that the specific tasks and activities may vary depending on the team and the context. However, the core responsibilities and accountabilities of each Agile Team member remain the same. Let us look at each individually.

Product Owner

The Product Owner (PO) is accountable for the product's outcome and for maximizing its value. His or her main responsibility is to translate the problem that we are trying to solve into a product solution that is valuable, feasible, usable, and viable. They should continuously be asking:

"Are we delivering outcomes to our end users, to our customers, and to our business?"

"Is the work that we are doing valuable?"

"Are the features and the functionalities that we have built, working for our customers?"

"Does the product that we have built solve the customer needs, or should we build something else?"

From a competency point of view, this role is typically aligned to the business or to the Product Management team because these people need to understand the business, the business strategy, and the business priorities. They also need to understand the customer in terms

34

of who the customer is, what the customer needs, and also the market in which the customer operates.

PRODUCT OWNER

Responsibilities:

Communicate effectively: Share the product vision, roadmap, and updates with stakeholders regularly, aligning everyone towards the same goal. Gather frequent feedback to guide product decisions.

Emphasize a customer-centric mindset: Put the customers at the heart of every decision, understand their desires, needs, and pain points.

Prioritize and refine the backlog: Order the backlog items based on their value and ensure they are clear and understandable.

Collaborate closely with the team: Work hand-in-hand with Team Members and other Product Owners to drive efficient product development.

Validate solutions: Build solutions iteratively, validate hypotheses, and measure value delivered.

Accountability: Value of the product.

Maximize the value of the product resulting from the work of the Agile Team.

As a member of the Agile Team, the PO translates all of this knowledge into work items and priorities for the team to work on. And so, one important artifact that the Product Owner manages, is the Team Backlog, where all of the different work items are represented, and where User Stories are represented. The Team Backlog contains all of the work that the Agile Team is going to do over time.

The Product Owner also contributes to the overall vision and to the overall roadmap of the product by collaborating with Product Management. Also, being a member of the Agile Team, the Product Owner collaborates throughout the Sprint with the other Team Members, for example, by being available to answering questions, to providing context, and by validating the work that is being completed.

When working with SAFe teams, I find it critical for Product Owners to be empowered and to work collaboratively with Product Management. They should not be considered the receiving end of top-down directives and be relegated to an execution role ("Here is a Feature: go and build it as I envision it"). Instead, they should collaborate with Product Management to understanding the problem and to devising possible solutions. The Product Owners should then validate the possible solutions before committing to a full build.

> *"Decentralize decision-making to the people who have the most information."*
>
> Peter Drucker

For the Product Owners to be successful, and for the product that they are building to be successful, it is important for them to be empowered to own the solution and to identify the best way for implementing it. A solution should not be dictated from the top. Instead, Product Owners should be given the context about a problem and key outcomes to deliver, and then be empowered to figure out how to build the best solution and to deliver the outcomes.

Marty Cagan calls this the Netflix principle[vi]:

> *"Push the decisions down to the people*
> *that actually have the knowledge to solve*
> *the problem."*

How they do this varies by the organization. But a key element of the Product Owner's job is to measure the value delivered. The Product Owner continuously measures the outcomes delivered, and they decide what to do next to improve the product.

In fact, at a minimum, Scrum offers an opportunity for the Product Owner to do just that. It is the Sprint Review, where the Agile Team meets with its stakeholders and with its customers. That is a great opportunity where they can get feedback on the outcomes delivered, and any additional expectations they may have.

For Product Owners to be successful with SAFe, they need to support the following responsibilities:

Customer Focus

- **Emphasize a customer-centric mindset:** Put the customer at the heart of every decision. Use tools like Design Thinking to understand their desires, needs, and pain points.

- **Gather frequent feedback:** Conduct interviews, gather data, and actively seek user feedback to guide product evolution.

- **Focus on value:** Prioritize features and initiatives based on their potential to deliver value to the customer and to the business.

Collaboration

- **Collaborate with Product Management:** Collaborate with Product Management and with other Product Owners to define the overall product vision, roadmap, and strategic priorities.

- **Validate solutions:** Build solutions iteratively, validating ideas and key hypotheses, and measuring value delivered. Collaborate with Product Management to define and to deliver MVPs.

- **Collaborate closely with the team:** Work hand-in-hand with Team Members to identify the best solutions to customer's problems, to drive efficient product development, and to build products to quality.

- **Collaborate with stakeholders:** Build strong relationships with key stakeholders, including executives, engineers, marketing, and sales. Share the product vision, the roadmap, and the updates with stakeholders regularly, aligning everyone towards the same goal. Solicit their input for feedback and for new ideas.

Vision and Strategy

- **Create a compelling vision:** Articulate a clear and concise vision for the product that inspires the team and the stakeholders. Align the vision to the broader vision for the full product. This vision should be constantly revisited and updated as needed.

- **Prioritize effectively:** Focus on delivering the features and the functionalities that provide the most value to customers and to the business. This includes supporting other teams' dependencies and iterating on possible solutions.

Agility

- **Embrace iteration and feedback:** Regularly gather feedback, adapt to changing needs, and refine the product roadmap based on insights.

- **Treat backlog as emergent:** View the product backlog as a living document, open to iteration and improvement, and not as a fixed plan imposed from higher levels.

- **Understand SAFe principles:** Familiarize yourself with the core principles of SAFe, including economic value, alignment, transparency, and continuous learning.

- **Practice self-improvement:** Continuously learn, grow, and stay updated on the latest trends and best practices in agile product management.

Scrum Master / Team Coach

The Scrum Master / Team Coach, in general, serves as a coach to the team. So, they are not expected to manage the work or to prioritize the work because that is what the Product Owner does. The Scrum Master acts as a coach to the Agile Team to help the Team Members better adopt Scrum and SAFe practices. They help the team to learn about these practices, to adopt them effectively, and to also help the team focus their work. Sometimes, the Team Members need a bit of coaching to keep the focus on what they are doing, and the Scrum Master can help with that.

For example, once the Team Members have selected a Sprint Backlog, they should focus on the work that needs to be done in order to execute the work in the Sprint. Not something else, not changes of priority, not the next shiny object, but:

"Let's keep the focus on what we are committed to doing so we can deliver value at the end of the iteration, and then maybe the next iteration we will change the priorities."

In essence, the Scrum Master helps the team to focus and to deliver value. The Scrum Master also helps the team to identify, to track, and (if the team needs help) to remove the impediments. Sometimes there are things that we need to do that we really do not know how to do. We may be stuck because we do not have access to the system or because we lack support from other teams. All of these could be impediments and the Scrum Master can help the team remove these impediments.

And then, especially in the context of SAFe when we have multiple teams working together, the Scrum Master is not just working inside the Agile Team; they also work across the various Agile Teams in an

ART (Agile Release Train) and across the organization. For example, aligning the work that they are doing with other Scrum Masters, or helping the rest of the organization understand how to better support the Agile Teams so that everybody can work in a better agile way within the organization.

SCRUM MASTER

Responsibilities:

Coach the Agile Team: Help the team understand and implement Scrum effectively.

Facilitate Scrum events: Ensure all Scrum events are held and followed correctly.

Cause impediment removal: Help to identify and resolve any obstacles that hinder the team's progress.

Promote continuous improvement: Help the team identify and implement ways to improve their processes and practices.

Accountability: Effectiveness of the Scrum Team.

Ensures the team is functioning effectively and delivering value.

The Scrum Master Is a Servant Leader

The Scrum Master / Team Coach is a servant leader for the Scrum Team, and for the Organization. The following points are freely elaborated from the Scrum Guide and represent some key responsibilities of the Scrum Master[viii]:

Service to the Scrum Team

The Scrum Master covers the following responsibilities towards the Team Members and the Scrum Team overall:

- Teach Scrum and guide in adopting Scrum, Agile, and SAFe practices.
- Coach on methods and techniques to improve quality of work delivered and engineering practices such as those that support the adoption of DevOps.
- Help the team identify and remove impediments.
- Help the team improve team productivity, effectiveness, and happiness, fostering personal and professional growth.
- Help in creating a strong Definition of Done.
- Facilitate Scrum events as needed to help the team achieve the objective of the event.

Service to the Product Owner

The Scrum Master covers the following responsibilities towards the Product Owner:

- Ensure that the PO shares context and vision with everyone on the Agile Team.
- Help the PO make the product backlog visible, ordered, dynamic, and clear to all.
- Help the PO learn techniques for effective product backlog management.
- Share priorities of the product backlog and reasons behind them.

- Coach the PO on techniques to properly learn about customer needs and reflect these in the product backlog.

Service to the ART and Organization

The Scrum Master covers the following responsibilities towards the rest of the ART and the broader organization:

- Coach everyone involved with the product development effort on the value of incremental and iterative product development.

- Drive change and help organizational impediments get removed in order to increase the productivity of the team.

- Work with other Scrum Masters and the RTE to coordinate change and increase the effectiveness of Scrum across the organization.

- Help the organization transition traditional roles in Project Management to roles in Scrum/Agile/SAFe.

- Coach stakeholders on the importance of attending Sprint Reviews and System Demos, and of actively providing feedback to the team.

- Help teams with the support needed to effectively work together and collaborate whether co-located or remotely distributed.

Because the Scrum Master is accountable for the Agile Team's effectiveness, their daily activities vary depending on the maturity level of the team with agile and SAFe practices. The Scrum Master Competency Ladder[ix] shows how the Scrum Master role evolves as the team matures and as the Scrum Master grows.

The Scrum Master competency ladder

LEARN TO FLY

Focus on the Scrum Team and Scrum framework

LEVEL 1

You help the team learn and adopt Scrum effectively.

ACTIVITIES
Facilitate Scrum events
Support the Product Owner in product backlog refinement
Guide the team to remove impediments and solve internal conflicts
Coach the team on Scrum Patterns

SPREAD YOUR WINGS

Work across multiple Scrum Teams and with other Scrum Masters

LEVEL 2

Your team runs almost on auto-pilot. You can expand your focus to other teams.

ACTIVITIES
Foster continuous improvement by partnering with other Scrum Masters
Cross-team facilitation and coaching
Community of practice
Coach the Product Owner on Product Patterns
Guide teams in adoption of technical excellence

REACH FOR THE SKY

Shift the focus onto the organization, its leadership, and its culture

LEVEL 3

You dedicate most of your time to helping stakeholders and leaders in the organization support Agile principles and empower Scrum teams.

ACTIVITIES
Identify and help solving culture impediments
Coach leadership on adoption of Agile principles
Engage stakeholders in supporting the Scrum teams
Coach the product leadership on Product Patterns
Facilitate workshops to support Product Management

Team Members

The third role is represented by the Team Members (in Scrum, they are called Developers). These are all of the people on the Agile Team who do the work selected for the Sprint. So, this is basically everybody else on the team other than the Product Owner and the Scrum Master. In general, in the Agile Team we may have a combination of software developers; we may have testers; and we may have designers, architects, people who do integration, and whoever needs to be on the team to be able to execute the work.

NOTE: The Scrum Guide uses the term "Developers" to represent Team Members. These terms are used interchangeably in this book. Also note that the PO and the SM are also members of the Agile Team.

Team Members Responsibilities

Their responsibility is **to build, to test, and to deliver** increments of functionality for the product, one Sprint at a time. At the beginning of the Sprint, they select the work to be done. During the Sprint, they do the work. And again, they build, they write the code, they test the code, and they make sure that everything works. If there are bugs or other things that show up, they fix these bugs. And by the end of the Sprint, whatever work they had committed to doing in the Sprint should be completed 100% so that it can be delivered to the end user or to the customer, if we want to do that.

Their responsibility is also to ensure that the product is **built with quality**. By the end of each Sprint, what the Team Members have built should satisfy the standards of quality for the product; there should be no bugs or technical debt, or other things that may impact the functionality of the system.

They have the responsibility to **remove impediments**. If they have impediments, they work as a team to try to remove them. Sometimes the impediments may be outside of the team, or they may not know how to remove impediments. So, they request help. And this is important because by asking for help, they can improve and move forward. The key person who can help is the Scrum Master, as we said earlier.

TEAM MEMBERS

Responsibilities:

Analyze, design, develop, test, and integrate product backlog items into potentially shippable increments.

Deliver potentially shippable Product Increments: Work together to complete the work in each Sprint, ensuring the Increment meets the definition of "Done" and is ready for release.

Self-organizing and cross-functional: Plan their work, estimate effort, and manage their own tasks within the Sprint.

Continuous improvement: Identify and implement ways to improve their processes and tools.

Accountability: Deliver working product.

Ultimately responsible for the quality and functionality of the product delivered in each Sprint.

And then, especially in the context of SAFe where we have multiple Agile Teams working together, an important responsibility of the Team Members is to sync up with other Team Members in other Agile Teams, especially when there are **dependencies**. They need to identify these dependencies and then go and talk to the Team Members in other teams to align on the work, to make sure everybody knows that you have a dependency on them, and that they can schedule their work to support what you need to accomplish.

DevOps Delivers Software Solutions Effectively

DevOps is a philosophy and set of practices that aims to improve the collaboration and communication between development (Dev) and operations (Ops) teams. Traditionally, these teams have functioned in silos, which can lead to slow development cycles, finger-pointing, and a hesitancy to release new features.

Here are some of the key benefits of adopting DevOps for development teams:

Faster releases: DevOps practices like continuous integration and continuous delivery (CI/CD) automate many of the tasks involved in getting code from development to production, including testing and integration. This can significantly speed up the release process and allow development teams to get new features into the hands of users faster.

Improved quality: DevOps emphasizes automation and testing throughout the development lifecycle. This can help to catch bugs and defects earlier in the process, resulting in higher quality software.

Increased collaboration: DevOps encourages a culture of shared responsibility and collaboration between team members and between different teams. This can lead to better communication and a more efficient development process.

Greater innovation: By reducing the effort spent on testing, integration, and deployment, DevOps allows development teams to focus on innovation and creativity. They can spend less time on manual tasks and more time on developing new features and functionality.

Improved morale: DevOps can lead to a more positive and productive work environment for development teams. By automating tasks and reducing errors, developers can focus on more creative work and have a greater sense of accomplishment.

Overall, DevOps can help development teams to be more efficient, effective, and innovative. It's a cultural shift as much as a technical one, but the benefits for development teams can be significant. SAFe teams employ DevOps practices for increased quality and collaboration.

How a Team Improved Its Approach Using DevOps

By Anil Jaising, CST, Certified DevOps Trainer

When I joined JP Morgan Chase in 2014, I was greeted with this quote by the Lead Development Manager:

"We work in a highly regulated environment, we have tight deadlines, and we have teams across the world. To ensure that we don't make mistakes, we need to build, test, and deploy manually. Our environment and situation are special, nothing like you might have experience elsewhere."

I was hired as a Transformation Coach to help the team, the product owner, and the stakeholders adopt better product management, Agile, and DevOps principles and practices.

As a coach, my job was to observe and help the team despite their current beliefs.

"A common disease that afflicts management the world over is the impression that our problems are different - They are different but the principles that will help to improve quality of product and service are universal in nature."

W. Edwards Deming

The product, being regulatory in nature, had to be released in production with new attributes, rules, and workflow once every

47

quarter. Working backwards, we started a new test release cycle a month before release in the UAT (User Acceptance Test) environment. The team worked on requirements gathering, development, QA testing every sprint (each sprint was two weeks long). Our larger team was split into six individual teams, two in New York, one in Glasgow, and three in India.

Cumulatively, the teams were working on six streams of work. Every week and a half, the developers integrated the separate codebases, merged them manually, and then tested them before involving the QA people on the team.

Each manual merge would take two days. Promoting code from the development environment to the QA environment required a lot of coordination. Sometimes the database would be ahead of the code. Sometimes the code base worked well in the developer's workstation or in the dev environment, but once the team moved it to QA, it would not work anymore. After several hours of debugging, the team would identify a fix and apply it manually to finally complete the merge.

Testing was performed by the members in the Scrum teams that had QA expertise. They identified bugs and then debated fixes with the coders back and forth like ping-pong balls.

In addition to the development challenges across many streams, testing cycles, and system integration, the team also struggled with requirements gathering. Product management was chaotic, with several handoffs between the stakeholders, the product management team, and the business analysts within the various Scrum teams.

As I observed these behaviors and challenges both in New York and in India, I started creating an idea of how to help these teams improve by using DevOps practices and principles.

In DevOps there are three core principles, and they are known as the "Three Ways":

The First Way: The Principle of Flow

Lead time is the time from which an individual request is made until that work gets delivered. Cycle time is the time from when the team starts working on the new request until it's delivered[x].

Large, complex organizations that work on tightly coupled, monolithic applications and use limited integration environments, typically require months of lead time. Their flow of work is slow, and they have limited ability to adapt quickly to changes in requirements.

"One of the major contributing causes of chaotic, disruptive and catastrophic software releases is the long lead time required to get to the releases, caused by siloed work performed by development and operations."

DevOps Handbook by Gene Kim

Many successful companies like Amazon, Netflix, Meta, and others have been able to increase the flow of work by limiting the work in progress, by delivering work in small batches, by reducing the handoffs that are typical with siloed functional areas in a large organization, and by making the hierarchy flat. This makes them different from traditional large complex organizations.

Ideally, developers receive fast, constant feedback on their work, which enables them to quickly and independently implement, integrate, and validate their code and to deploy their code into production. They do this continuously, deploying small batches of work. Fast feedback is the goal, and smooth flow of work from development to operations allows to deliver value to the customers quickly.

To implement this principle, work needs to be visualized using value stream mapping or impact mapping so that the specific issues can be identified and fixed. I considered visualizing the whole system as one value stream, but quickly realized that such a large-scale change would likely be resisted.

"Choosing a value stream for DevOps transformation deserves careful consideration."

DevOps Handbook by Gene Kim

I first chose to ensure that we could configure and create server environments on the fly. This was the low-hanging fruit to help the team reduce the overall delays and hence the lead time. We created different configurations and a script that would pick the required configuration and build the server environment on the fly. By versioning the configuration, we ensured that we could completely destroy an environment and build it from scratch in an automated way.

Seeing the positive impact of the infrastructure improvements, I was able to secure budget for a full-time engineer to support other value streams. With the additional capacity we were able to build a continuous integration and delivery pipeline using Jenkins and Gitflow.

Our next challenge was to get the databases in each environment in sync. We used a tool to keep the databases in sync, destroy and load the database in every environment on the fly.

Finally, we took a proactive approach to build unit and automated functional testing. We built an entire delivery pipeline weaving the development, the testing, the database, and the infrastructure so we could deploy on the fly in every environment.

The Second Way: The Principle of Feedback

Failure is inherent and inevitable in complex systems, whether in manufacturing or technology. When a problem is detected in one component, it is often difficult to isolate the other components. It also defies a single person's ability to see the system as a whole and understand how all the pieces fit together. So, creating fast feedback loops is critical to achieving quality, reliability, and safety in the technology value chain.

We hooked up the tools we used for versioning, for quality testing, and for continuous integration and deployment, to an open-source telemetry solution called Hygiene.

This started providing Developers and Operations staff real time view into the entire delivery cycle and allowed us to enable quality gates so that we could stop the pipeline on the first sign of trouble (very similar to an Andon Cord used by the Toyota manufacturing teams to stop the production when there is a problem).

The Third Way: The Principle of Continuous Learning and Experimentation

This principle encourages a culture of continuous learning and experimentation within DevOps teams. By constantly trying new things and measuring the results, teams can improve their processes and deliver better products faster.

The Third Way also supports a culture of sharing: Lessons learned from experiments and failures are openly shared within the team and organization. This helps to prevent others from making the same mistakes and accelerates collective learning.

Our local discoveries spread. We documented and promoted the learning from this work across the firm. This led to other teams hiring engineers and adopting similar ideas. DevOps started to become a company-wide practice.

In a couple of years, the firm created a continuous integration and delivery product that every team adopted firm-wide.

Watch videos, find additional resources, and learn more by following the QR code.

An Effective Scrum Fuels an Effective SAFe

Because SAFe is dependent on Scrum (and to some extent, on Kanban) it is useful to refresh some key concepts about the Scrum workflow. Typically, Agile Teams use Scrum to plan and to execute the work in Sprints, with a typical duration of each Sprint of 2 weeks. Some teams may use Kanban instead of Scrum, and the SAFe framework allows Scrum and Kanban teams to coexist.

The actual work of developing a new product or service is done at the Team level. The Team level is composed of Agile Teams. It is the foundation of SAFe and is essential for the success of any SAFe implementation.

In fact, it is pretty much impossible for a scaled organization to adopt SAFe effectively if its teams struggle with adopting Scrum effectively in the first place. A robust Scrum implementation is a necessary condition for scaling with SAFe (or with any other scaling framework, for that matter) so it is useful to spend some time on ensuring that the Agile Teams are adopting Scrum effectively (the same is true for teams adopting Kanban).

Learn More

To refresh your knowledge of Scrum, visit www.trulyscrum.com.

Scrum Workflow

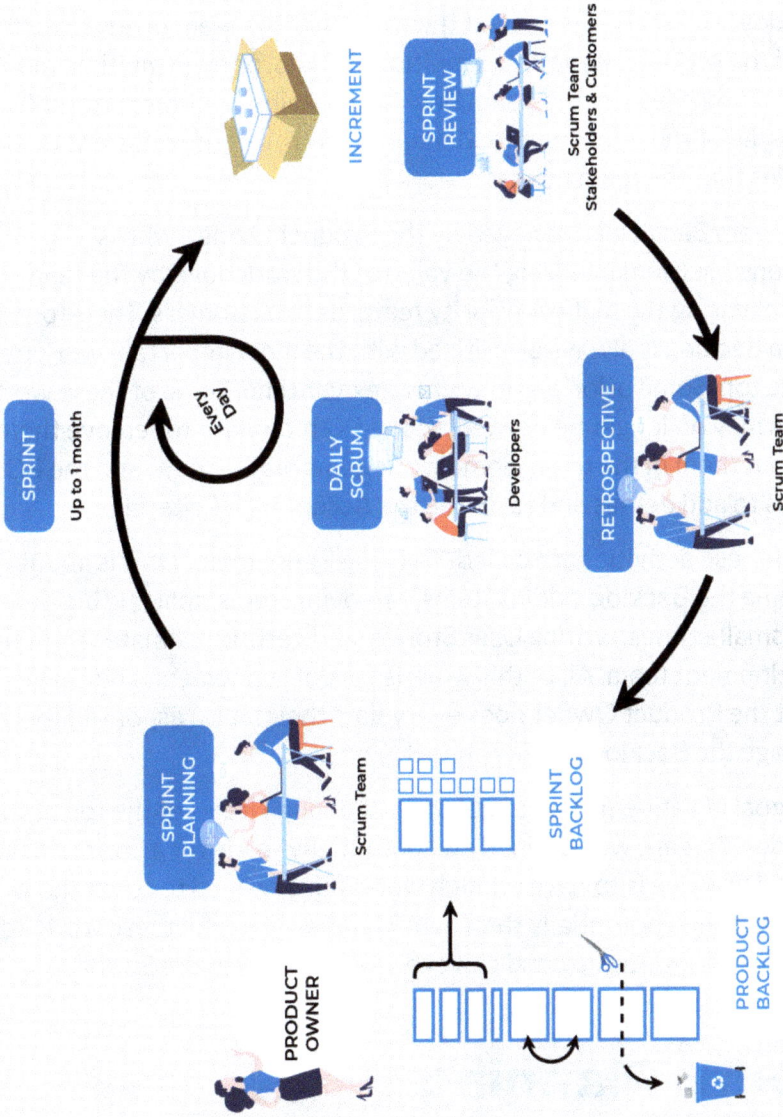

SCRUM MASTER

SPRINT
Up to 1 month

Every Day

INCREMENT

SPRINT REVIEW
Scrum Team
Stakeholders & Customers

DAILY SCRUM
Developers

RETROSPECTIVE
Scrum Team

PRODUCT OWNER

SPRINT PLANNING
Scrum Team

SPRINT BACKLOG

PRODUCT BACKLOG

53

Team Backlog and Refinement

For a given Agile Team, in Scrum, all of the work starts from the Team Backlog. In the picture, it represents the first artifact on the left, and it can be called interchangeably the Product Backlog or the Team Backlog. This is the list of all of the work that the team needs to do to build the product. It may take multiple Sprints, or even multiple months to be completed. So, the Team Backlog contains all of the different work items, all of the different functionalities, and all of the different User Stories that the team needs to work on.

The Team Backlog is managed by the Product Owner, who is responsible for maximizing the value of the work done by the team and for delivering the highest priority features to customers. Therefore, the Team Backlog is always prioritized with the most important work items at the top. Some priorities may change over time. Some of these work items may no longer be needed, so the PO may want to remove them and put them in the trash. Some work items may be new, and the PO needs to add details and to define the Acceptance Criteria.

All of these activities are called "Backlog Refinement": this is about refining the Backlog, adding items, removing items, splitting big items into smaller ones, writing User Stories, and getting estimates from the development team. All of this work is part of refinement, and that is what the Product Owner does every day: their main responsibility is to manage the Backlog and to refine it.

The goal of refinement is to get at least enough items at the top of the Backlog that are well defined and potentially ready for a Sprint. In fact, a good practice is to have enough work items refined to cover the next 2 to 3 Sprints: potentially the Team Members can pull these work items into the Sprint Backlog and can execute the work in the Sprint.

Sprint Planning

When the team starts a new Sprint, the first thing to do is Sprint Planning. The objective is to plan the work that the team is going to execute in the Sprint, represented by the Sprint Backlog.

"How much work can we commit to doing this Sprint?"

First, the Team Members assess their available capacity for the upcoming Sprint. Typically, they start by looking at past performance (the amount of work they have completed in prior Sprints, also called Velocity). The available capacity may be reduced by vacation days, by official holidays, or other events that cause people to be unavailable for work (for example, someone may get married and leave for honeymoon). So, you need to account for all of these to establish what is the available capacity that you have.

Once they know the available capacity, the Team Members can pull from the Team Backlog the list of work items that they can do in the Sprint within that capacity, and they create the Sprint Backlog. It is important that the Team Members define the plan for the Sprint within their available capacity to avoid overcommitment.

Team members are expected to complete 100% of the work they select for the Sprint Backlog. This establishes a commitment for the Sprint and allows for proper planning (e.g., setting release dates that can be reasonably met).

"What is a buffer?"

A buffer is a portion of capacity that we do not plan and that we leave unplanned to cover for something unexpected that may happen in the Sprint. It decreases the available capacity and crates a safeguard against overcommitment or to deal with unexpected events. For example, we may get a priority bug. We may get a production issue. We may have a Team Member who gets sick during the Sprint, and now we lose capacity.

To account for these unexpected events, we leave a buffer that we do not plan, and a typical buffer is 10% to 20% of Velocity. If you have an average velocity of 25 points per Sprint, 20% of that represents 5 points that you can leave for the buffer. That means that the available capacity for the Sprint is 20 points.

NOTE: these are starting values. You may want to choose the right amount of buffer for your team based on the type of work you do, and the number of unplanned events that you may need to deal with in a Sprint. Some teams need a larger buffer to deal with more unpredictable work requests.

Calculating Velocity and Capacity

Every team needs to establish its own capacity for each Sprint. Capacity is the amount of work that a team can do in a Sprint. Velocity is the amount of work that is completed in a given Sprint.

A good way to establish capacity is to use our historical Velocity to see how much work we have been able to complete in prior Sprints; that gives us a baseline for how much work we can expect to complete in the upcoming Sprint. While different Sprints may have different Velocities, we take the average Velocity[xi] of the last 3 to 5 Sprints to minimize variability. We use that figure to establish the capacity for an upcoming Sprint.

"How do the Team Members establish the available capacity for the Sprint?"

In this example, the team has already completed three Sprints. From the picture, you see that in each Sprint they completed a list of stories, and that each story had a specific story point estimate. So, when we look at the first Sprint, and we add up the amount of work completed, Sprint 1 had a Velocity of 13 points and Sprint 2 had a velocity of 16 points.

Sprint 3 is a bit tricky. They had originally committed to 18 points, but at the end of the Sprint, story N was not completed. They only did 50% of the work. So, story N does not count toward the Velocity: there is no partial credit because the story was not done. Therefore, in Sprint 3, the Velocity was 13 points.

At the end of the Sprint, a Story can only be in two states: it is either "Done" or "Not Done"[xii]. Therefore, any work item that is not 100% completed, does not receive any partial credit and returns to the backlog.

Available capacity for the Sprint

You have completed 3 sprints:

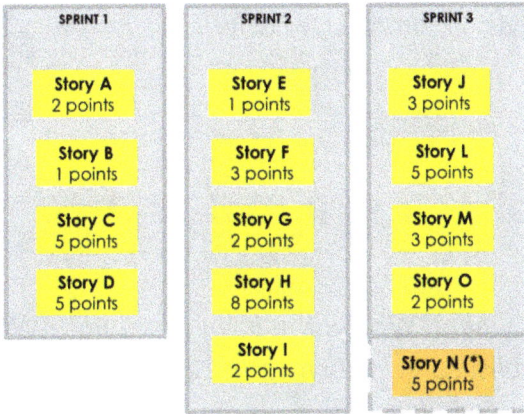

SPRINT 1	SPRINT 2	SPRINT 3
Story A 2 points	**Story E** 1 points	**Story J** 3 points
Story B 1 points	**Story F** 3 points	**Story L** 5 points
Story C 5 points	**Story G** 2 points	**Story M** 3 points
Story D 5 points	**Story H** 8 points	**Story O** 2 points
	Story I 2 points	**Story N (*)** 5 points

- **Sprint 1** had a velocity of ___13___ **points**
- **Sprint 2** had a velocity of ___16___ **points**
- **Sprint 3** had a velocity of ___13___ **points**

(*) Story N was completed only 50%

Average velocity
(over the last 3 sprints)

14
POINTS

We can calculate capacity for Sprint 4:

SPRINT 4

BUFFER

Available capacity for Sprint 4:

11
POINTS

20%
3 POINTS

Now, if we take the average of these 3 Sprints, the average is 14 points. It is called **average Velocity**.

We can go in Sprint 4 and start calculating the available capacity. In theory, we know that we can do 14 points in a Sprint (from our average Velocity). However, it is a good practice to establish a buffer.

Learn More

Visit https://www.5dvision.com/post/velocity-capacity-load to learn more.

How to Baseline the Initial Team's Velocity

"What if we are a new team? What if this is the first Sprint? We do not have any established Velocity measure. How do we create an estimate for our capacity?"

There are different techniques that you can use to baseline your initial capacity, for example:

Run a Sprint and measure amount of work completed: Run the first Sprint by pulling a number of PBIs (Product Backlog Items) and by getting as many done until the Sprint is over. Then, measure the amount of work completed: this is your Velocity for Sprint 1, and now you have a baseline for the following Sprints.

Use a normalized approach for your first Sprint: Establish a baseline for your team's capacity using a normalized approach that equates a story point to time or to people. Run your first Sprint, then use Velocity moving forward.

The SAFe normalized approach for the initial team's capacity

SAFe suggests a normalized approach to define your initial capacity based on a starting number of points per Team Member. The advantage of this method is that you can start planning a series of Sprints in a PI without having completed one in the past. The limitation is that this is an artificial expedient and is not based on the team's actual ability. Nonetheless, it gives new teams a baseline to start planning their work.

The technique works like this:

1. Count the number of Team Members on your team. So, for example, if you have 3 software developers and 2 testers, you have 5 Team Members. Notice that the PO and the SM do not count.
2. Assign 8 points to each Team Member[xiii]. So, if you have 5 Team Members, you have a total of 40 points available.
3. Decrease the total number by any working days that any Team Member is going to miss in the Sprint (remove 1 point per day per Team Member). For example, if a federal holiday is going to fall in the middle of the Sprint, everyone will be out of the office. So, you lose 1 point per Team Member, for a total of 5 points in our example.
4. The remaining total of 35 points is the available capacity for your team at Sprint 1.

This method gives you a starting point for the available capacity in your team. However, you should consider this like it is, a starting point. This is a technique you should use for the first Sprint, when you do not have past performance, and therefore you do not have an established Velocity. This is just a way for you to get started. After you complete your first Sprint, you will have actual Velocity, and now you can use this measure for the capacity of your Sprints.

"Is it really true that a person can do 1 point per day?"

No, it is not true. It may not be true, ever. It may not be true for everybody. It may not be true for all of the teams. This is just a way to get started with an initial baseline.

After you have completed Sprint 1, you can look back and see how much work the team actually completed in Sprint 1. That number, the actual work completed, is your team's Velocity, and that becomes your team baseline for the next Sprint.

So, after Sprint 1, when you get into Sprint 2 and so on, you should forget this technique. You do not want to keep the "8 story points per Team Member" rule. Instead, you can now use past activity (your actual Velocity) as a measure for your team's capacity.

Tips for an effective Sprint Planning

A successful Sprint Planning event begins with proper preparation. Before the meeting, ensure you have all necessary information, including a well-refined Team Backlog, priorities for the work items, input from the ART Backlog about Epics or Features to prioritize, and alignment to the roadmap. You may also want to review any dependencies between Stories in the Team Backlog, and any dependencies with other teams.

Here are some suggestions and tips for conducting an effective Sprint Planning in SAFe:

Start with purpose: Begin by reviewing the goal of the Sprint and by reminding participants of the overall PI Objectives or Product Goal you have defined. This creates alignment among Team Members on the overall goals and objectives.

Define acceptance criteria: Clearly define acceptance criteria for each selected Story to ensure everyone understands what "done" looks like. Factor the acceptance criteria in the estimation of each Story. This can be done during refinement or at Sprint Planning.

Identify risks and dependencies: Discuss potential risks and dependencies that may impact the Sprint and develop plans to mitigate them. If you have external dependencies, be prepared to sync up with the other team as soon as possible (or even better, invite the PO or a key representative from the other team to participate in your Sprint Planning event).

Consider team capacity and availability: Confirm capacity with the Team Members rather than telling them what their capacity should be. Ensure they account for vacations, for commitments, and for potential dependencies outside the team.

Daily Stand Up / Daily Scrum

Every day of the Sprint, the Team Members do the work on those work items selected in the Sprint Backlog. To help the Team Members achieve the goal and complete all of the work by the end of the Sprint, they do the Daily Stand Up (in the Scrum Guide, this is called the Daily Scrum).

Typically done in the morning, every day, the Daily Scrum is an opportunity for the Team Members to sync up with each other, to look at how they are doing the work in the Sprint, and to look at what is missing so that they can deliver the whole Sprint Backlog by the end of the Sprint.

The Team Members check their own progress and then decide what to do next to move forward and to deliver the whole Sprint Backlog. This is a conversation between the Team Members, and it is useful for them to sync up and to decide what to do next.

The Role of the Team Members at Daily Scrum

The key to a successful Daily Scrum is to understand its purpose. The goal of the Daily Scrum is to align on the progress of the Sprint and answer these questions:

"Where are we with the work we have committed to doing in this Sprint?"

"What tasks are we going to complete today?"

"What impediments may prevent us from achieving the goal of the Sprint?"

To answer these questions and create alignment with everybody, the Team Members should do the following during Daily Scrum:

- Look at the Sprint Burn-down chart to get a quick glance at where they are in the Sprint.

- Look at the team board (the team's Kanban board), and in particular at the PBIs in the "Doing" or "Testing" columns.

Discuss what to do today in order to move forward and possibly complete these items.

- Jot down a list of impediments and decide a time later in the day when they will meet to review them and do problem-solving activities.

The Role of Product Owner at Daily Scrum

The Product Owner is optional at the Daily Scrum because this event is not to provide a status update to them (it is for the Team Members to sync up). However, it could be useful for the Product Owner to participate for context. They can listen to the conversation between the Team Members to get a sense of what is going on with the team and to offer any help.

The Product Owner may suggest a time later in the day to meet with the Team Members, to answer questions, or to discuss requirements. This can be a "Follow up meeting" or "PO office hours".

The Role of Scrum Master at Daily Scrum

The Daily Scrum is a conversation between the Team Members, hence the Scrum Master is optional.

Sometimes the team is relatively junior in doing Scrum and they may not know exactly how to do the Daily Scrum or how to do it effectively. So, the Scrum Master, acting as a coach, can help the Team Members with a structure and with some facilitation, so that they learn how to do the Daily Scrum. Maybe they do this for a few days; maybe they do this for a Sprint or two. At some point, the Team Members will learn how to do the Daily Scrum. At that point, the Scrum Master does not need to be there anymore – or at least, they don't need to actively facilitate it anymore.

Even for a mature Scrum team, it may still be useful for the Scrum Master to attend the Daily Scrum to make sure that the Team Members do it right, or to jot down a list of impediments to help the Team Members solve them later in the day.

Tips for an effective Daily Scrum / Daily Stand Up

Here are a few tips to for the Team Members to keep the Daily Scrum focused and effective:

Focus on the Sprint goal: Keep the discussion focused on the current iteration's goals and how individual tasks contribute to them. Review progress toward the goal and discuss how to get there.

Use a visual board: Utilize a physical or digital Kanban board to visualize the workflow and progress of Stories and tasks throughout the Sprint.

Review the Burn-down chart: Update the Burn-down chart before Daily Scrum and then review it together to understand if you are on track to complete all the work by the end of the Sprint, or if any changes are needed.

Focus on updates, not problem-solving: While acknowledging impediments, briefly discuss and potentially identify solutions, but avoid lengthy problem-solving within the Daily Scrum. Schedule follow-up time for problem-solving discussions later in the day.

Sprint Review

On the last day of the Sprint, the team organizes the Sprint Review with key stakeholders and customers. The purpose of this event is to present what the team accomplished during the Sprint and get feedback to decide what to do next on the product.

By the time they are ready for the Sprint Review, the Team Members should have completed the work that they originally selected for the Sprint. It means that they have created an Increment of their product.

"What is an Increment?"

It is basically the result of the work that they have done in this Sprint. It can be considered the deliverable that they have produced in the Sprint.

At Sprint Review, the Agile Team presents its increment to the stakeholders, to the end users, and to the customers. They present the increment, and they say,

"Look, this is what we have accomplished in this Sprint. Can you please use it? Test it. Tell us if it is the right thing for us to do. Is there anything missing, or anything that we should change? Give us some feedback."

And then, based on the feedback that it gets from stakeholders and from customers, the team may decide what to do next. There could be new priorities, new ideas, new features, or new functionalities, maybe some enhancements to existing features. And they take these ideas and put them into the Product Backlog for their evaluation and possible prioritization for a future Sprint.

To ensure the Sprint Review is productive, the Product Owner should be familiar with the team's achievements, challenges, and the functionality of the increment beforehand. This requires an ongoing interaction with the Team Members throughout the Sprint, including inspecting, reviewing, and providing feedback on the work done. The Sprint Review should not be the first time the PO sees the increment.

The essence of Sprint Review is for the Agile Team to get feedback on the work that it has done, and then decide what to do next.

Sprint Review is also an opportunity to share and discuss the overall plan for the product. For example, the PO can discuss the progress in the PI towards the PI Objectives, share updates on the PI Burn-up Chart (read more in an upcoming chapter), and discuss the next steps in the roadmap. These conversations help the participants be aligned on the status of the project, and on the expectations of what is coming up next.

System Demo

In SAFe, because we have multiple teams working together on the same product, the Sprint Review may be replaced with the System Demo. The concept is the same, it is just that the System Demo is done by all teams together, where each team presents its updates and work accomplished. This saves stakeholders' time compared to doing multiple Sprint Reviews, and also allows stakeholders to experience an integrated view of the product at once.

To leverage the presence and participation of stakeholders, don't limit the System Demo to a series of presentations about what teams accomplished. Instead, use the System Demo to collect feedback from stakeholders about what works well and what needs improvement; to discuss where you are compared to the PI Objectives you have defined for your team; and, to align stakeholders on any plan updates, including changes in priorities or in the roadmap.

Tips for an Effective Sprint Review/System Demo

Here are a few tips to keep the Sprint Review or System Demo focused and effective:

Focus on completed work: Showcase the Stories and functionalities that the team completed during the Sprint, not what they couldn't finish. Only work that is 100% completed should be part of the Increment.

Demonstrate, don't just present: Use live demos to engage stakeholders and allow them to interact with the completed work. Even better, let the stakeholders use the product you have built and let them discover problem areas or things that need improvement.

Share and discuss updated plans: Provide a high-level update on the priorities in your backlog and discuss any updates to the roadmap. Gather input from stakeholders to help you make decisions on what to do next on the product.

Update the Team Backlog: Collect suggestions and new ideas from the participants, and add them to the Team Backlog. Mark them as "needing discovery or validation". Later, plan on collecting data and on performing discovery activities to decide whether to continue the work on these ideas and how to prioritize them.

Celebrate success: Acknowledge the Team Members' achievements and celebrate their progress towards the Sprint goal.

The Product Owner is not a stakeholder: The Product Owner is a member of the Agile Team. Hence, they have a direct responsibility in what gets built during the Sprint.

Sprint Retrospective

At the end of the Sprint, the team does the Sprint Retrospective. This is an internal meeting within the Agile Team and only within the Agile Team. Which means the Product Owner, the Team Members, and the Scrum Master. So, there are no external people, no customers, no stakeholders, no management, and nobody else. It is only the Agile Team.

And the purpose of the Retrospective is to look at how we work together as a team and to identify opportunities for improvement. The team may discuss these questions:

"What are our relationships, our communication channels, and our processes? Do we feel empowered? What gets in the way of doing great work? Do we feel like a happy team or maybe not?"

"And so, what can we do so that we get better as a team?"

The Retrospective can be a powerful event to help the team improve. Here are a few suggestions:

- Change the exercise or the list of questions every Sprint. Do not run the same Retrospective over and over.

- Focus the Retrospective on something specific, rather than "the last sprint." For example, do a Retrospective on how the team is implementing the 5 Scrum values. Or do a Retrospective on the communication between the Product Owner, the Developers, and the stakeholders.

- During the Sprint, the Scrum Master can jot down a list of pain points and challenges he or she observes for the team. Then, at Retrospective, can suggest focusing the discussion on a specific observation.

- Identify one or more action items (things you can do to improve as a team) and put them in action as soon as possible, ideally immediately in the next Sprint.

Tips for an Effective Sprint Retrospective

When the time comes to conduct the Retrospective with the team, consider these tips:

Establish psychological safety: Foster a safe and open environment where team members feel comfortable expressing their opinions and concerns without fear of judgment.

Ensure that the Product Owner participates at Retrospective: The Product Owner is a member of the Agile Team. Hence, they should participate at Retrospective together with the other team members.

Focus on solutions, not blame: While acknowledging challenges, shift the focus towards identifying actionable solutions and preventative measures for future iterations.

Develop an action plan: Create a specific and actionable plan with clear owners and timeframes for implementing agreed-upon improvements. A Retrospective without action items is a waste of time.

Communicate and track progress: Share the actions taken since the last Retrospective and regularly monitor progress toward completing the action plan.

Consider rotating the facilitator role: This can encourage team engagement and diverse perspectives.

Planning is key, avoid winging it: A good Retrospective requires preparation. This is typically the job of the Scrum Master, but the team can contribute. A day or so before the event, plan how to conduct the upcoming Retrospective reflecting on:

- **Set the stage:** Choose a comfortable and conducive environment for open and honest discussions.
- **Gather feedback:** Collect observations throughout the Sprint and prepare to share at Retrospective. Encourage pre-

retrospective anonymous input through surveys, tools, or prompts to gather initial thoughts and stimulate reflection. Decide one or two activities to collect further input during the Retrospective.

- **Define the focus:** Align with the team on the specific areas of discussion. Do not just discuss "How did the last Sprint go?" but select an area of focus. This could be based on challenges faced, areas for optimization, or broader improvement objectives.

PI Planning

The PI Planning Event

PI Planning is also known as Big Room Planning in other contexts. While SAFe didn't invent Big Room Planning[xiv], it made it a core part of its framework. It is a collaborative planning event that brings together all teams and stakeholders who are involved in a large project or ART. It is typically held once a quarter in order to plan the upcoming work and to ensure that everyone is aligned on the goals and on the objectives.

During PI Planning, teams review the overall roadmap and break down the work into smaller, more manageable sections. They then estimate the effort that is required for each section of work and prioritize it, based on the overall goals. Once the work has been prioritized, teams create a plan to determine how they will collaborate so as to complete the work within the allotted time frame.

PI Planning is a cornerstone of SAFe and is a valuable tool that is utilized to improve communication, collaboration, and alignment among teams. It also helps to identify and to mitigate risks early on, and to ensure that everyone is working toward achieving the same goals.

Here are some of the benefits of Big Room Planning:

Improved alignment and communication: PI Planning brings together all of the teams and stakeholders who are involved in a project, which helps to ensure that everyone is aligned on the same goals and objectives. It also provides an opportunity for teams to communicate with each other and to learn about each other's work.

Reduced risk: PI Planning helps teams to identify and to mitigate risks early on. By reviewing the overall roadmap and by breaking down the work into smaller sections, teams can better understand the challenges they face and then to develop plans to address them.

Increased efficiency: PI Planning helps teams to be more efficient by identifying and by eliminating waste. By working together to plan the work, teams can identify and avoid potential bottlenecks and dependencies.

Improved quality: PI Planning helps to improve the quality of work by ensuring that all of the teams are working toward the same goals and objectives. It also provides an opportunity for teams to review each other's work and align on dependencies.

The goal is to invite all of the Agile Teams on an Agile Release Train (ART) to come together in one large room, to spend a couple of days to look at the plans, to define the objectives, to identify dependencies, and to create the plan for the upcoming quarter. This can be a high energy kind of event, as you can imagine, when there are about 100 - 120 people all together in one large room, talking with each other, aligning on the plans, identifying dependencies, and negotiating timelines.

At the end of the 2 days, every team will have identified a plan for the next 4 to 6 Sprints (for the next PI). And they will have identified the list of dependencies that they have with other teams to incorporate into the plan and to make sure that everybody can work together and move forward.

SAFe offers a wealth of resources to schedule and to organize PI Planning[xv]. A good starting place is the online documentation available at: www.scaledagileframework.com/pi-planning.

Planning Interval

As we discussed before, a PI (Planning Interval) is a period of 4 to 6 Sprints (8 to 12 weeks). Very often, a PI is associated with a quarter (3 months). A PI is a fixed period of time, during which an Agile Release Train delivers a working increment of value. PIs are used in SAFe to coordinate the work of multiple Agile Teams and to ensure that they are aligned on a common goal.

NOTE: Prior to SAFe 6.0, the PI was defined as a Program Increment.

Planning Interval (PI) and PI Planning

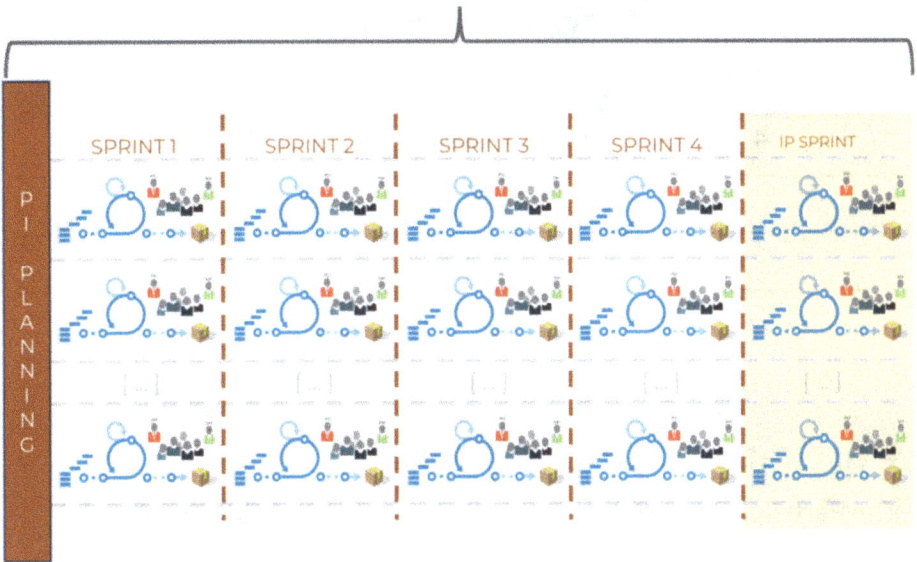

At the beginning of a PI, PI Planning helps the teams align their plans for the upcoming Sprints in the PI.

In this picture, you can see an example of a PI that covers 5 Sprints. Teams plan the work that they will do in a PI at the PI Planning event. Then, they spend the next Sprints doing the work and delivering the objectives they had initially planned. Once a PI is completed, the teams do another PI Planning and start the next set of Sprints. Each PI has the same duration (same number of Sprints) so as to establish a regular cadence for planning and for delivering work.

During PI Planning, the teams define and align their plans for the upcoming PI. The plan spans 4 to 6 Sprints (you should decide between 4, 5, or 6 Sprints. A shorter PI provides greater flexibility. Many organizations opt for the longer duration of 6 Sprints because it aligns with quarterly planning).

Once you have established the duration of a PI, teams can plan their work for the number of Sprints they have available in the PI. Typically, the Sprints available are all except one: the last Sprint is considered an Innovation and Planning Sprint, also called the IP Sprint. Visit the chapter on the Foundations of the SAFe framework to learn more about the IP Sprint.

Number of Sprints in the PI	Number of Sprints available for doing work in the PI	Number of IP Sprints in the PI
4	3	1
5	4	1
6	5	1

Participants in PI Planning

The Participants in PI Planning include a number of different people.

At a minimum, they include all of the Agile Teams working together on the same Agile Release Train. And when I say Agile Teams, I mean, the Product Owners (POs), the Scrum Masters (SMs), and every Team Member on all of the teams. That is why this is really a Big Room kind of event.

Additional teams may participate. Often, these are horizontal teams, those that are providing support to all the other teams. The typical example is a System Team, that is providing development support or integration support to the other teams in the ART. Or another example could be the UI/UX (User Interface/User Experience) team, a dedicated team for UX design and UX research.

It could be very useful to invite these teams to participate at PI Planning because other Agile Teams may have dependencies on the System Team or on the UI/UX team.

Product Management also participates, and this could be the Product Manager at the ART level, Epic Owners at the Portfolio level, or people like the Chief Product Officer (different organizations refer to this role in different ways). In general, these are the people who provide oversight at the higher level for the product that the teams are building, including the product vision and overall priorities.

The System Architect is there to provide the overall direction for the architecture of the system.

The RTE (Release Train Engineer) is responsible for organizing and for facilitating the overall PI Planning event, including all of the different activities. The RTE is supported by the Scrum Masters of the Agile Teams, who have the responsibility to help each team move forward and to do the PI Planning activities.

And then the leadership team, or the executives, may participate in PI Planning. Their role is to provide overall strategy and vision for what we are trying to achieve. And, toward the end of PI Planning, they listen to the readout from the different teams and provide feedback on the overall plan for the PI.

Inputs and Outputs of PI Planning

Let us look at a typical structure of a PI Planning event.

"What are inputs that we need to prepare before PI Planning? What are the team activities? What are the outcomes they will generate with PI Planning?"

Inputs to PI Planning

In terms of inputs, to be able to run PI Planning, we need at least a couple of items. The first one is the ART Backlog, and in particular, the list of high-level priorities that we need to deliver in the upcoming PI. It could be Features or some low-level Epics that we need to focus on for the next PI.

And then the product vision: it's important to share the vision and overall objectives we are trying to achieve.

During PI Planning

While doing PI Planning, the teams are going through several activities.

For example, they need to estimate capacity. Then based on that, the teams plan the Sprints.

"What work can we do in each Sprint?"

To be able to do that properly, they need to have a Team Backlog that is refined. Sometimes, the teams need to spend a bit of time during PI Planning to refine their backlog. The team members get aligned on the work, estimate each of the work items, and identify any dependencies.

Sometimes you have dependencies on other teams and you are going to call out these dependencies. You can walk over to the other team and say,

"Hey, look guys, I have a dependency on you. Can you please add this work to your own Team Backlog, to make sure it gets done on time for when I need to get my own work done?"

And that means communication. There must be communication throughout PI Planning not only within the team, but also between all of the other teams.

At the end of the PI Planning event, the teams are going to take a confidence vote to share how confident they feel about the plan that they have put together.

Outputs of PI Planning

At the end of PI Planning, each team has a plan for each of the Sprints in the upcoming PI, with a list of dependencies that they have on other teams, and dependencies they need to support from other teams.

The teams also have a list of objectives – called PI Objectives – that they commit to deliver by the end of the PI, and a list of risks that could be in the way or prevent them from achieving those objectives.

A Real Story: More Work Done in Just One PI

I would like to share a real-life story about the benefits of doing PI Planning.

A few years ago, I supported an organization that was doing very complex work. The teams were building a large internal system, and they were already a couple of years into development with multiple teams working together. Unfortunately, they were struggling.

74

There was a poor alignment between different teams. When they had dependencies, there was no structured approach to identify, to track, and to solve these dependencies, so teams were waiting forever to get a dependency completed by another team. Nobody knew where they were relative to the overall plan, as there was a lack of focus and a lack of priorities. Priorities were continuously changing.

As a result, **it was extremely challenging for any team to get any work done.**

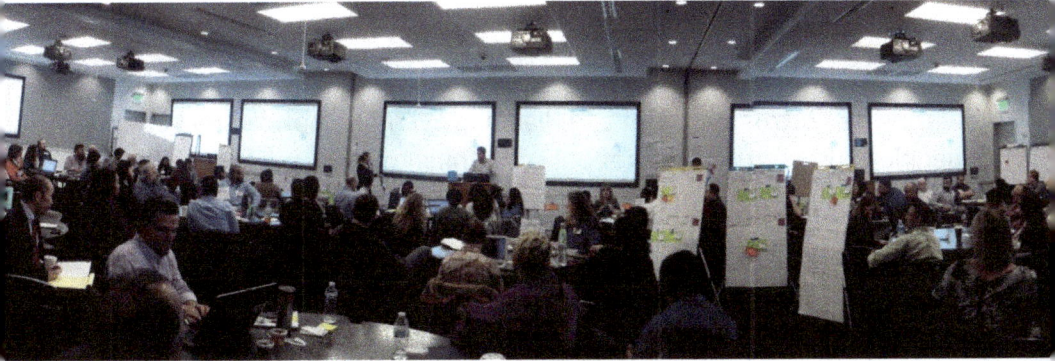

PI Planning event with 120+ people in one big room

The organization asked for help in implementing SAFe. That is when we came onboard, and we helped organize the first PI Planning with all of these teams (about 125 people in total). Once they had put together their plan for the PI, the teams then executed the 6 Sprints in the PI. And, when they were done, they came back for our second PI Planning event.

During that second PI Planning event, the executive in charge of this project was in the room. At the beginning of the day, she went to the podium, and she shared that in the prior PI – the one the teams had just completed:

> *"The teams had been able to complete more work in just that PI, than in the prior year that they had been together."*

That was an amazing realization on their part, and an understanding that all of the work they had put into PI Planning was worth it. The comradery, the alignment, and the communication that the teams got during PI Planning, enabled them to be more effective and enabled them to focus on what really mattered. As a result, the teams improved their productivity and their effectiveness. It was clear that everyone felt elated by this achievement.

These are the benefits that teams can achieve by doing this work properly, by spending time in a Big Room Planning, by aligning their dependencies, by making their plans, and by defining objectives.

A Real Story: PI Planning Retrospective

During the Retrospective at a PI Planning event, we noticed that a few people expressed concerns about something that was perceived as impactful and negative. When we asked for deeper insights, we learned that the teams were wasting a lot of time trying to figure out dependencies with other teams.

Because this was a new organization, some of the teams did not know each other, and they could not figure out who was there to help with the dependency, or which team they should go and talk to. They were wasting a lot of time going around the room asking and looking for those teams.

So, out of this feedback, we came up with an idea. At the next PI Planning, on each table, we put a large balloon and a big sticker on the balloon with the team's name. That made the team's name visible from everywhere across the room. In addition to the team's name, we added the core specialty of each team.

After we did that, if anybody was confused, they could just look around at the different balloons and find the right team in a much more efficient way.

Creating a Plan for the PI with the Team Board

PI Planning is an intense and high-energy event where each Agile Team establishes a plan for the PI and aligns it with the other teams for dependencies. To support the teams in crafting their plans, each team has what is called a Team Board. This is a space that the team uses to create a plan for the Sprints in the PI, to define the objectives, and to identify the risks.

A Team Board is typically divided in multiple sections:

- One section for each Sprint that you need to plan. So, there is Sprint 1, Sprint 2, Sprint 3, etc.
- A section for the PI Objectives.
- Another section for the risks.

Using the Team Board, the team performs the following activities:

Activity #1: Load the Sprints with Stories and Create a Plan for the PI

List the Stories you Plan to Do Each Sprint

The team selects and assigns Stories to specific Sprints to create a plan for the upcoming Sprints. This activity is called "loading the Sprints".

The Stories come from the Team Backlog and are selected in order of priority established by the Product Owner, or based on technical dependencies that the team needs to consider in executing the work. The Stories may include any new priority determined by Product Management during PI Planning, and any technical debt work or Enabler.

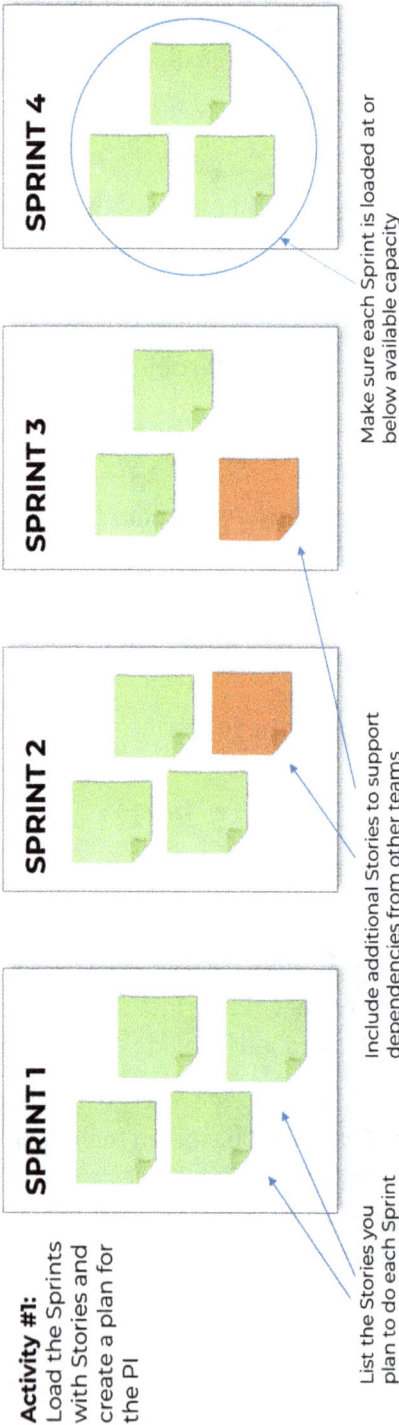

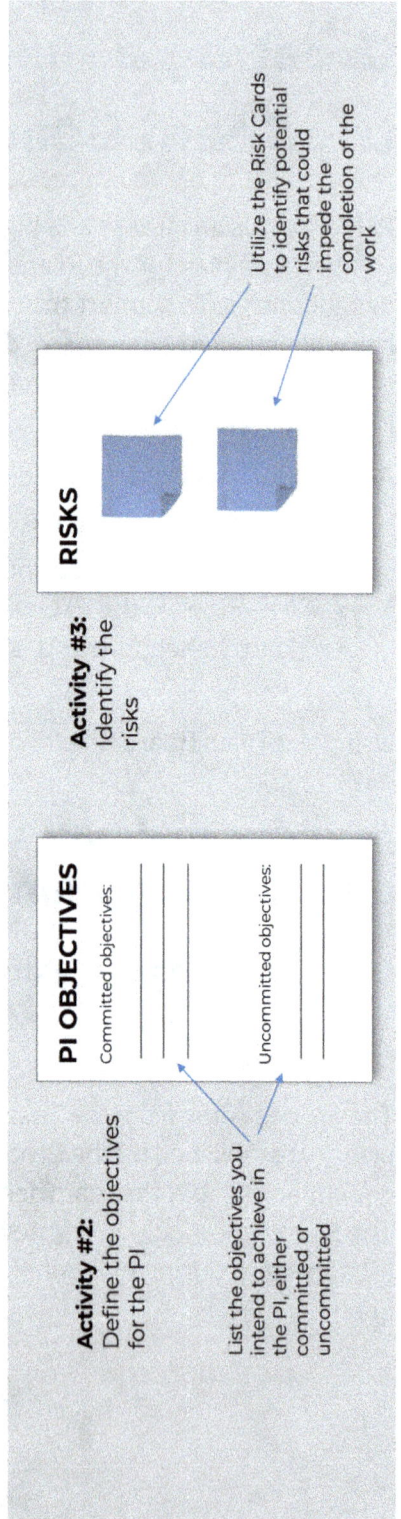

SPRINT 1 **SPRINT 2** **SPRINT 3** **SPRINT 4**

Make sure each Sprint is loaded at or below available capacity

Include additional Stories to support dependencies from other teams

List the Stories you plan to do each Sprint

Activity #1:
Load the Sprints with Stories and create a plan for the PI

RISKS

Utilize the Risk Cards to identify potential risks that could impede the completion of the work

Activity #3:
Identify the risks

PI OBJECTIVES

Committed objectives:
_____
_____
_____

Uncommitted objectives:
_____
_____

Activity #2:
Define the objectives for the PI

List the objectives you intend to achieve in the PI, either committed or uncommitted

Typically, we start with loading Stories into Sprint 1 until the Sprint is full. Then, we move to Sprint 2, then Sprint 3, and so on. As a result, we create a plan for each of these Sprints.

This plan, of course, is looking ahead. It is in the future. However, this plan is not set in stone. We create it based on the knowledge that we have today, to reflect what we intend to do in the upcoming Sprints. It may be subject to change as we learn more about the work, as new work shows up, or simply as we validate the solutions and decide to make changes to the plan.

Consider this: creating a fixed plan for multiple Sprints and then being prohibited from making updates contradicts agile principles, wouldn't you agree?

Include Additional Stories to Support Dependencies from Other Teams

Because we work in a scaled agile configuration with multiple teams working on the same product, it is very likely that we may have dependencies with other teams. These dependencies may go either way:

- **We depend on another team to get some of our work done:** When we depend on other teams, we need to call these dependencies out. We need to go and talk to the other teams, explain what we need from them, and ask them to support us.

- **Another team depends on us to get their work done:** The other team has a dependency on us, and we have extra work to do to support them. This extra work needs to be added to our plan.

You should discuss all dependencies with the other teams and post them on the ART Planning Board: This is a useful tool to visualize all the dependencies within the ART (see the next section).

Make Sure Each Sprint Is Loaded at or Below Available Capacity

During PI Planning, one of the first steps for each team is to determine the capacity for each Sprint in the PI (to do this, follow the procedures we discussed earlier for Sprint Planning).

Then, as you load the Sprints, ensure that the total load does not exceed the capacity of the Sprint. If it does, you risk setting unreasonable objectives and risk over-committing. It is better to establish reasonable plans that fit within the available capacity. You can always change the plan or add more work later once you have completed what you had originally planned.

Activity #2: Define the Objectives

List the objectives you intend to achieve in the PI. These objectives represent what you intend to achieve in the PI and should be related to the work that you have planned in the Sprints.

For more information on PI Objectives, see later in the book.

Activity #3: Identify the Risks

Utilize the Risk Cards to identify potential risks that could impede the completion of the work. Risks may be of different kinds, some may be controllable, others cannot be mitigated. It is useful to call out the risks that may prevent you from successfully complete the work in the PI, and potentially find ways to mitigate their impact.

For more information on Risks and the Risk Card, see later in the book.

Updating the ART Planning Board

The ART Planning Board (prior to SAFe 6.0 it was called Program Board) is a useful artifact that teams can use to identify, highlight, and track dependencies they have with other teams. They update the ART Planning Board during PI Planning as new dependencies are identified and the corresponding work needs to be mapped into each teams' plan. The ART Planning Board helps to answer the question:

"When we have multiple teams working together on the same product, how can we organize the work across all of the teams including dependencies?"

This can be quite a complex and daunting task especially when there are many dependencies between multiple teams.

Thankfully, PI Planning offers that opportunity because we are all in the same room creating a plan together. In addition, the ART Planning Board allows us to track the dependencies, create transparency, and align on the plan.

NOTE: Starting in SAFe 6.0, the Program Board is called the ART Planning Board. I use both terms interchangeably.

Let me first explain the structure and then we can look at how to use it:

- At the top, in the first row, you have the iterations or the Sprints. So, that would be Sprint 1, Sprint 2, Sprint 3, and so on.
- The second row is typically any external events that we need to track. For example, major events happening in the marketplace, or some major milestones that we want to highlight.
- And then we have one row for each team in the ART. In this example, we have the Spider-Man team, the Doctor Strange team, the Mystique team, and so on. These are all of the different teams in the train.

- At the bottom, we have some additional teams; these are the support or horizontal teams, for example, the UX team or the System team.

ART Planning Board

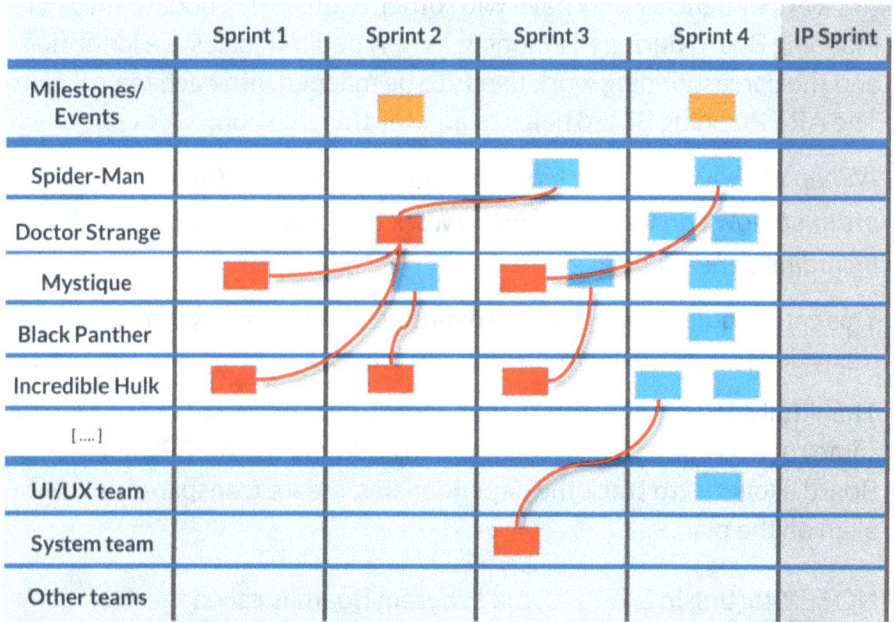

	Sprint 1	Sprint 2	Sprint 3	Sprint 4	IP Sprint
Milestones/ Events		🟧		🟧	
Spider-Man			🟦	🟦	
Doctor Strange		🟥		🟦 🟦	
Mystique	🟥	🟦	🟥 🟦	🟦	
Black Panther				🟦	
Incredible Hulk	🟥	🟥	🟥	🟦 🟦	
[....]					
UI/UX team				🟦	
System team			🟥		
Other teams					

Color	Meaning
Orange	Milestone/ Market Event
Blue	Feature completed
Red	Significant dependency

Red String = A dependency requiring Stories or other dependencies to be completed before the Feature can be completed

Now that we have this structure, let us look at how we use the board. The idea is that, as a team works on its plan for the PI and schedules the work for each Feature, it is placing a card on the ART Planning Board to signal in **what Sprint the team intends to complete** the specific piece of work. The blue card identifies the completion of the work on a specific Feature.

Features are placed on the board with these rules:

- The row indicates the team doing the work.

- The column is the Sprint where you plan to complete the work on the Feature.

- Notice that we put Features on the ART Planning Board, not Stories. This is to reduce clutter and to really focus on delivering end-user functionalities.

- The dependencies are placed on another team's row to signal to them what you need them to do, and they are typically called out with a red card connected with a string to the Feature that depends on that red card.

For example, the Spider-Man team is communicating that it will complete its first Feature in Sprint 3 by putting a blue card in the corresponding column on the board. However, the Spider-Man team has a red string attached to it that leads to a red card placed in the Doctor Strange team's space in Sprint 2. With that string connection, the Spider-Man team is communicating that it has a dependency on the Doctor Strange team. And the Spider-Man team is requesting that the Doctor Strange team completes its work on the red card by Sprint 2. Therefore, the Doctor Strange team needs to add this dependency to its own plan for Sprint 1 or 2.

Let us look at the red card in the Doctor Strange team space. The Doctor Strange team has 2 additional dependencies; 1 is on the Mystique team, and 1 is on the Incredible Hulk team. These 2 dependencies are represented on the board with 2 more red cards, connected with a string to the card that is dependent on them. Each of these dependencies need to be finished in order for the Doctor Strange team to do their part of the work.

The ART Planning Board as a Diagnostic Tool

An ART Planning Board can be considered a snapshot of the team topology within an ART: it shows how the teams are structured in relation to each other and what the dependencies between the teams are. Used as a diagnostic tool, it can help you identify problems with the team topology and possibly evaluate how to restructure the teams to simplify the topology.

An ideal ART Planning Board has just a few dependencies: this means the Agile Teams have a considerable degree of independence from each other, are cross-functional, and are able to deliver their objectives without depending on other teams.

When building complex products, the reality is often different. As much as we strive to create cross-functional teams that can independently deliver work, because of the scale of the organization, teams have dependencies that need to be addressed.

This ART Planning Board shows the complexity of team inter-dependencies.

As the teams organize their work and identify their dependencies, the ART Planning Board gets populated with red cards connected by red strings. You can look at the board and get a feeling of the overall well-being of the ART.

The ART Planning Board becomes a diagnostic tool that helps to visualize the complexity and interdependencies between teams.

For example, the ART Planning Board pictured here illustrates a complex web of dependencies between just a few teams. It represents a snapshot of the team topology at that moment.

When these teams realized it, they called for a break in PI Planning and discussed how to reduce the number of dependencies. As a result, they decided to make changes to the team composition, re-assigning team members and updating the team topology.

After restarting PI Planning, the teams ended up with a noticeably more efficient plan with fewer dependencies between them.

Tips to Manage the ART Planning Board

Let me share a few tips on how to use the ART Planning Board:

TIP 1: Talk to the other teams.

Putting a red card on another team's space and connecting it to your card with a string, it is a good starting point, but it is not enough. You also need to walk to the other team and say,

"Look team, we need your help. We have this dependency on you, and we need for you to complete all of this work in Sprint 1, so that as a result we can do our work in Sprint 2 and get it done. Can you support us?"

This conversation is very important, and it is what creates transparency and alignment between the teams. This is an ongoing communication between every team to identify dependencies and to make sure that all of the different dependencies get accounted for. In the end, we do PI Planning all together so that we can have this type of conversation between different teams!

TIP 2: Dependencies Should Not Be Vertical

When you have dependencies on another team, it typically takes time for the other team to complete their work before you can start your own. So, when you map out the dependencies on the ART Planning Board, you want to make sure that the red string goes backward. This gives the other team time to complete the work before you need that dependency done.

ART Planning Board

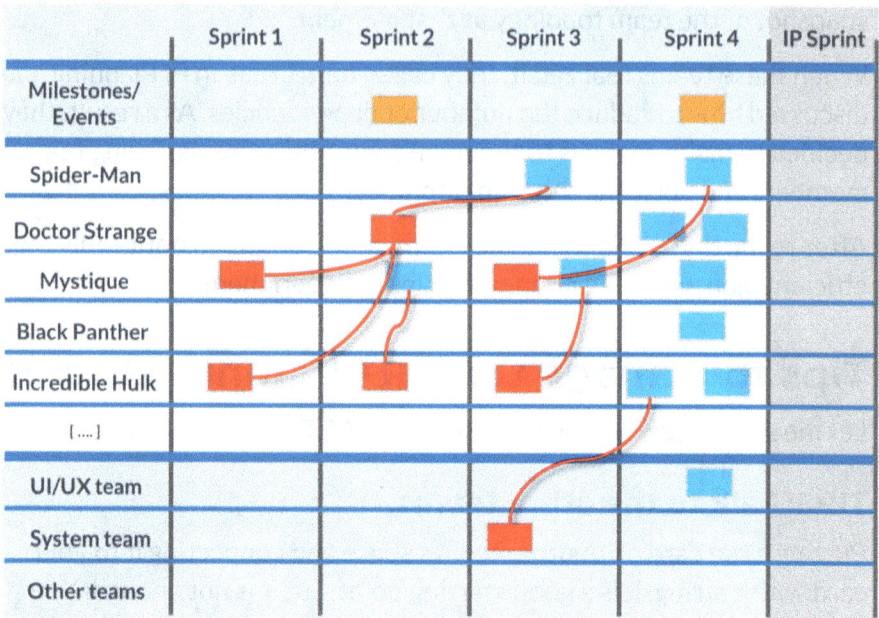

	Sprint 1	Sprint 2	Sprint 3	Sprint 4	IP Sprint
Milestones/Events		🟧		🟧	
Spider-Man			🟦	🟦	
Doctor Strange		🟥		🟦 🟦	
Mystique	🟥	🟦	🟥	🟦	
Black Panther				🟦	
Incredible Hulk	🟥	🟥	🟥	🟦 🟦	
[....]					
UI/UX team				🟦	
System team			🟥		
Other teams					

Orange — Milestone/Market Event

Blue — Feature completed

Red — Significant dependency

Red String = A dependency requiring Stories or other dependencies to be completed before the Feature can be completed

Instead, if you have a dependency that goes down vertically on the same Sprint, it is risky. The risk is that if the other team completes its part of the work by the end of the Sprint, then you have no time to actually complete your work in the same Sprint, so your Feature may not get done. For example, the Mystique team has two vertical dependencies (same Sprint) with the Incredible Hulk team.

You always want to check that a dependency goes backward, because it gives time for a team to complete its own work, and then you can complete your work in the next Sprint.

TIP 3: Watch Out for Back-load of Your PI

You may notice that in the picture of the ART Planning Board in the previous section, 6 of the 11 Features planned by the teams for the entire PI are all scheduled to be completed in Sprint 4 (the last working Sprint in the PI). For example, the Doctor Strange team is planning to deliver 2 Features this PI, and both are scheduled for the last Sprint. The Incredible Hulk team has a similar plan.

This means that the plan for the PI is heavily back-loaded, increasing the risk that some of these Features may run late and may slip to the following PI. This is a particular concern when there are many dependencies between the teams: you just need a few of these to slip, and many of the Features planned for the PI will not get done.

If that is the case, invite the teams to re-think their plans and to find ways to distribute the work on the Features more evenly throughout the PI. If there are dependencies, make sure that the teams have accounted for these dependencies in their Sprints to avoid delays.

TIP 4: The Scrum Master Guides the Team Members

The Team Members are responsible for updating the ART Planning Board. So, the Team Members should be walking to the board and be placing the cards on it, because they know the details, they know the dependencies, and they know what the work is all about. And they are also responsible for communicating with the other teams so that the other teams can incorporate the changes into their own Sprint plans.

Notice that this is an active role of the Team Members, who are working together and communicating with each other. The Scrum Master is responsible for making sure that Team Members do this. The SM should invite the team members to go to the ART Planning Board, call out dependencies, and go talk to the other teams.

One good way to do that is to invite the Team Members to go to the ART Planning Board and make sure that it is updated. This could be prompted every hour during PI Planning. The SM can also set up a timer to remind everyone when it is time to do so.

Manage the Business Effectively with SAFe

By Thomas Nowaczyk, VP Product Management

I wanted to share some insights on the implementation of SAFe (Scaled Agile Framework) that I've gathered over the years. While SAFe offers a structured approach to aligning different agile teams, it's essential to ensure its implementation avoids resembling a traditional waterfall process. Here are my observations:

1. PI Planning serves as an excellent platform to outline collective goals and dependencies across the organization.

2. However, one of the challenges arises when plans need adjustment due to client or market feedback, or when new projects emerge as priorities. Agile methodologies excel in handling such changes, but PI cycles may struggle to accommodate them, especially when organizations rigidly measure teams against PI objectives. This inflexibility not only affects individual teams but also impacts the overall agility of the organization.

3. My advice to those embarking on the SAFe journey is to remember the primary focus: managing the business effectively. While PI efficiency metrics have their place, they should not overshadow the core objectives of generating revenue and solving customer problems. Embrace the fluid nature of agile processes and be transparent about deviations from the initial plans in your reports.

Ultimately, the goal is to keep progressing forward, utilizing SAFe as a valuable but imperfect tool. However, it's crucial not to become overly fixated on KPIs at the expense of flexibility and adaptability.

What Helps Teams Be More Productive or Effective?

By Ajiri Ideh, RTE, SPC

I have found that although there is guidance on how much preparation is "okay" for teams to have ahead of PI Planning, in reality, the advice for one team could be different for other teams. I found that some teams who work on products that have little to no dependencies on other teams are better able to have a "good" plan during PI Planning with little upfront preparation.

Conversely, some teams cannot produce any sort of plan without getting input from external teams or different Lines of Business (who sometimes require weeks of upfront notice). You would usually find this situation in hybrid organizations where an ART exists surrounded by Waterfall teams. In such cases, teams need to put in a lot more upfront work to get the information they require to plan appropriately.

Another scenario where one cap doesn't fit all is where you have a fairly large Scrum team. In a situation like this, the time a right-sized team needs to plan during PI Planning will be far less than what the larger team needs. Such large teams would need to put in some more upfront work in terms of reviewing their features, and the level of readiness of their stories.

The Role of the Product Owner at PI Planning

The Product Owner plays a crucial role in PI Planning, ensuring that the team develops the right features to achieve business goals. Overall, the Product Owner acts as the bridge between business needs and technical execution during PI Planning and later during the execution of the work. They bring valuable product expertise, guide feature development, and ensure alignment with strategic goals, ultimately contributing to a successful PI.

The Product Owner's responsibilities start before the PI Planning event begins to ensure that there is alignment with Product Management on the priorities in the PI. Then during PI Planning, the Product Owner supports the team in properly planning the work for the PI. And finally, after PI Planning and throughout the PI, the Product Owner supports the team in executing the work.

Let us breakdown the different responsibilities of the Product Owner:

Before PI Planning

- **Collaborate with Product Management:** They collaborate with Product Management, stakeholders, and clients to prioritize Features that deliver desired business outcomes; to define high-level objectives for what we are trying to achieve with the product; and to refine the product vision and the roadmap.

- **Communicate the product vision and the roadmap:** The Product Owner communicates the vision and roadmap to the Agile Team during PI Planning. This creates alignments and shared understanding among the team members.

- **Prepare the Team Backlog:** The PO ensures that the team backlog is well-organized and refined, containing high-level user stories prioritized for the upcoming PI. The goal here is not to have a fully refined plan for the PI (this will be created at PI Planning with the team). Instead, the goal is to have enough of an understanding of what can possibly be done in a PI, in terms of Features, high level user stories, and important priorities. The PO provides this input to the team members at PI Planning, and this helps to refine the plan for the PI.

During PI Planning

- **Educate the Agile Team:** The PO presents the product vision, the roadmap, and the key features to the Agile Team, ensuring that everyone understands the goals and priorities.

- **Guide user story creation and estimation:** The PO works with its teams to break down Features into Stories, to clarify acceptance criteria, and to estimate effort using story points.

- **Set PI Objectives:** The PO collaborates with Team Members to define PI Objectives, measurable statements aligned with the overall vision and the roadmap.

- **Help the team identify risks:** The PO collaborates with the team members, and other POs, to identify possible risks that may affect the execution of the work during the PI.

- **Facilitate collaboration and resolve dependencies:** They work with other POs to understand inter-team dependencies and to identify potential roadblocks, ensuring smooth collaboration throughout the PI.

- **Collaborate with Product Management:** Throughout PI Planning, the POs meet regularly with Product Management to sync up on progress, to clarify requirements for Features, to align on priorities, and to share updates on their plans. This PO Sync meeting also serves the purpose of identifying dependencies and make sure they are accounted for in the plans.

Throughout the PI

The Product Owner's job does not end with PI Planning, and instead continues throughout the PI to support the team in the execution of the work.

- **Refine the Team Backlog:** The PO continues prioritizing the backlog, refining user stories based on new information and feedback. The plan created at PI Planning may be updated with new work should priorities or dependencies change throughout the PI.

- **Participate in team events:** They attend and contribute to team events like iteration planning, reviews, retrospectives, and syncs, providing valuable product insights and feedback.

- **Track progress and report metrics:** The PO monitors progress toward PI Objectives and reports key performance metrics to stakeholders.

- **Inspect and adapt the plan:** At the end of each iteration, during Review or System Demo, the Product Owner collects inputs and feedback from stakeholders and customers, and uses these insights to make decisions on the plans moving forward.

- **Refine and re-prioritize the Team Backlog:** As new information come up, as the team collects feedback from stakeholders, and as new priorities emerge, the Product Owner updates the Team Backlog. Consequently, the plans for the upcoming iterations may be updated.

Consider this question:

"Who can really predict what will happen over the next 2 or 3 months with accuracy?"

A PI represents a (relatively) long stretch of time, typically between 2 and 3 months. The plan created for the iterations during PI Planning is a projection in the future of what the team expects to do, one iteration at a time. Considering this plan as a fixed commitment and not allowing for changes during the PI is a recipe for disaster.

One of the Agile values states[xvi]:

> *We value more responding to change over following a plan.*

Having a plan is important, and that is why the teams spend time at PI Planning to create one. However, the plan created at PI Planning at the start of a PI should be considered a guiding light, and not set in stone. If new priorities emerge during the PI, if markets or competition conditions change, or if stakeholders and customers provide new feedback to the Product Owner, the plan should be updated.

Any update to the plan is reflected into updates to the Team Backlog, to the plan of the iterations, and to the roadmap. Then, the Product Owner needs to create transparency with Product Management, with the stakeholders, and with other Product Owners by sharing the updated plans and the roadmap.

How Can the POs Support or Prepare the Teams for an Effective PI Planning?

By Brian Schweickert, SPC

I have found in my experience that a team who has their PO there 100% of the time will have a better plan and higher confidence than teams that do not. Be there for the entire time ... participate, be open to adjustments, offer clarifications, answer question, etc.

By John Mulligan, SPC

Product Owners should be working closely with the Product Management team to make sure that Features are ready well enough in advance of PI Planning to allow for the teams to begin the refinement process.

Seeing a Feature for the first time in PI Planning most often leads to disastrous results.

Teams should prepare for PI Planning starting about a month in advance. It should always be the goal of a good agile team to have a backlog of about 2 iterations worth of stories. As a result, about two iterations before the end of the PI, a team should have all its stories refined for the remainder of the PI.

That means it's incumbent on Product Management to have Features ready a month before PI Planning so that the POs can take those to the team to start refining.

With that said, do not over prepare. It's counterproductive to refine all four iterations worth of stories before PI Planning because that defeats the purpose of collaboration during the event.

Teams should prepare for PI Planning starting about a month in advance. It should always be the goal of a good agile team to have a backlog of about 2 iterations worth of stories. As a result, about two iterations before the end of the PI, a team should have all its stories refined for the remainder of the PI.

That means it's incumbent on Product Management to have Features ready a month before PI Planning so that the POs can take those to the team to start refining.

With that said, do not over prepare. It's counterproductive to refine all four iterations worth of stories before PI Planning because that defeats the purpose of collaboration during the event.

The Role of the Scrum Master at PI Planning

"What is the role of the Scrum Master during PI Planning, and what is the difference between a Scrum Master and an RTE?"

During PI Planning, the Scrum Master has a very important and active role. They do not do the planning. They do not do the work that the Team Members need to do. They do not identify the dependencies, plan the Sprints, or make trade-off decisions on what to do. None of these are the Scrum Master's responsibilities. However, they have an active role in making sure that the Team Members and the PO do all of this work and do it properly.

The Scrum Master *guides* the Product Owner and the Team Members to:

- Make decisions on the capacity for the Sprints
- Properly refine the Team Backlog
- Provide estimates for the Stories and PBIs (Product Backlog Items)
- Identify priorities within the Team Backlog
- Update the ART Planning Board
- Talk to other teams for their dependencies and incorporate the dependencies into their own plans.

Notice the difference between *guiding* and *doing*. The Scrum Master does not "do." They "guide" the Team Members so that they "do" and do it properly. And if the Team Members are not "doing," the Scrum Master should invite them to "do" these activities.

As I said earlier, one tip to do that, is to invite the Team Members to go and talk to the other teams, or to go to the ART Planning Board and to update it. The SM can set a timer every hour to remind the Team Members to do that.

Another thing the Scrum Master can do to guide their team is to ask questions like:

"Team, have you considered...?"

Or

"Where are you on this...?"

The Scrum Master at PI Planning

By Ajiri Ideh, RTE, SPC

The Scrum Master ensures the Scrum team is prepped and available for PI Planning. During PI Planning, they are responsible for the breakout room activities, ensuring the team is staying on track to completing their deliverables, and synchronizing with the RTE. Where external/

supporting representatives are required, e.g. Architects, they schedule and invite these individuals in a timely manner, ensuring the team is not blocked. They make sure the team is planning with the right capacity/velocity.

They also resolve other impediments that come up during the planning.

By Brian Schweickert

#1 Be the timekeeper to ensure the team has a good draft plan on day 1 & final plan on day 2.

#2 Remember they are the servant leader of the team and focus on facilitation, progress, balance depth/breadth, continually gauge confidence in the plan, and get the Business Owners to participate with the team.

The Coach Sync During PI Planning

The Scrum Master also has another important role during PI Planning, and that is to sync up with the other Scrum Masters and with the RTE.

Typically, every hour or so during PI Planning, the RTE calls all of the Scrum Masters in a corner of the room and they do a Coach Sync meeting. This is an opportunity for the Scrum Masters to check in and to align with each other, making sure that all of the teams are moving along at the same pace, doing their work, planning dependencies, and so on.

If a team is stuck or does not know how to move forward, the Scrum Master can solicit the help of other Scrum Masters. Maybe another Scrum Master can go to the team and help move things along. Sometimes, a different perspective is all that people need to get unstuck.

The RTE guides the Coach Sync conversation by asking a set of questions to the Scrum Masters, by checking on progress, and by looking for impediments. The RTE typically has a booklet (like a reference document) for what questions to ask at each Coach Sync meeting. Scaled Agile provides a reference document with the recommended questions on its SAFe Studio website[xvii].

The Role of the Team Members at PI Planning

The Team Members (in Scrum, they are called Developers) play a vital role in PI Planning, contributing their technical expertise and their insights to ensure a realistic and achievable plan for the upcoming Planning Interval. Here are some key responsibilities:

- **Collaborate in refinement:** Team Members collaborate with the Product Owner to refine User Stories and Acceptance Criteria. They estimate the effort required for each Story, considering technical complexity, amount of work, uncertainty, and dependencies.

- **Define and adjust the plan:** Based on their estimates and on the available capacity in each Sprint, the Team Members adjust their working plan for each Sprint within the PI. This ensures that the plan aligns with the team's capacity and avoids over-commitment. By participating in the planning process, they take ownership of the plan and become accountable for delivering its commitments.

- **Identify and track dependencies:** Team members actively participate in identifying dependencies with other teams. They collaborate with team members in other teams to properly plan dependencies and to make sure the Sprint plans account for the extra work needed to support the requests from other teams.

- **Update the ART Planning Board:** Team Members update the ART Planning Board with the Features that they intend to deliver and the dependencies that they have on other teams. They sync with and collaborate with other teams to create alignment and transparency on these dependencies.

- **Identify risks:** Team Members identify possible risks and collaborate with the Product Owner to evaluate the impact of these risks. This early identification allows for proactive mitigation strategies and for improved collaboration.

- **Draft PI Objectives:** Developers contribute to defining PI Objectives, which represent the specific goals they aim to achieve in the PI. This fosters ownership and commitment within the team.

- **Align architecture and technical design:** In scaled organizations, the architecture of a complex system emerges from the teams doing the work. The System Architect oversees alignment and overall direction for the architecture and collaborates with the Team Members to define the details of the architecture.

Overall, developers play a crucial role in ensuring that PI Planning results in a realistic, achievable, and technically sound plan for the upcoming PI. Their contributions are essential for delivering valuable solutions and for achieving the desired business outcomes.

These traits are important for the Team Members to be successful:

- **Sharing expertise and knowledge:** Developers share their technical knowledge and insights with other teams during PI Planning. This facilitates cross-functional collaboration and ensures that everyone understands the technical implications of different Features.

- **Building relationships:** PI Planning provides a valuable opportunity for Developers to build relationships with other teams and stakeholders. This fosters better communication and understanding throughout the PI.

- **Ownership:** Team Members own their plans for the Sprints and for any decisions on available capacity. This ownership supports commitment to the plan and to the overall PI Objectives identified for the PI. This means the plans cannot be imposed by the Product Owner (or by other stakeholders) but are always created and committed to by the Team Members.

- **Technical excellence:** The Team Members are responsible for delivering quality work each Sprint. They foster technical excellence by supporting each other and by adopting technical practices like DevOps.

But their responsibilities do not end with PI Planning. In fact, the Team Members are pivotal in the successful delivery of solutions, each Sprint. The Team Members update their plans throughout the PI to reflect any changes in priorities, in dependencies, or in capacity. These updated plans are shared with the entire Agile Team and with its stakeholders at the earliest opportunity, to maintain alignment and transparency.

Team Members seek opportunities for continuous improvement as individuals and as a team. They participate in Retrospectives together with the Product Owner and with the Scrum Master, and suggest improvements to the development process, tools, and practices to enhance efficiency and quality of the product.

At the end of each Sprint, the Team Members integrate the work they have completed with the Increments from other teams, and participate in the System Demo. Here, they demonstrate the working solution to the stakeholders, collect their feedback, and update the plans for the upcoming Sprints as needed.

The Role of the ART Leadership Circle at PI Planning

By Vikas Kapila, SPCT, AKT, JMT

By now, you might have recognized the significance of the PI Planning event within the SAFe framework. This event typically extends over two days and engages essential participants including product owners, scrum masters, agile teams, stakeholders from different segments of the enterprise, as well as those managing upstream/downstream dependencies and the leadership circle of the Agile Release Train (ART).

The leadership circle of the ART for a PI Planning event typically consists of several key roles working together to facilitate the planning process and ensure alignment with organizational objectives. These roles include:

Release Train Engineer (RTE): The RTE serves as the facilitator and orchestrator of the entire PI Planning event. They coordinate with various teams, stakeholders, and leaders to ensure that the planning process runs smoothly and efficiently.

Product Management: Product managers represent the business stakeholders and are responsible for prioritizing features and defining the product vision and roadmap for the upcoming PI.

System Architect/Engineering: System architects or system engineers provide technical leadership and guidance, ensuring that the architecture and design decisions support the goals of the PI and align with the overall enterprise architecture.

Business Owners: Business Owners represent the interests of the business or customer, providing input on priorities, requirements, and market trends to inform the planning decisions.

Overall, leadership circle plays a central role in guiding and empowering teams during the PI Planning event, driving alignment, collaboration, and successful execution of the plans. The energy during the event is typically high, starting with anticipation and excitement as teams come together to discuss goals and strategies. There's a sense of focus and urgency as participants engage in discussions, share insights, and negotiate priorities. As the event progresses, the energy remains dynamic, with teams working towards consensus and making decisions that will shape the upcoming period of work.

Throughout the event, there's a palpable atmosphere of collaboration and commitment as teams work towards a common vision. Towards the end, there's a sense of accomplishment as plans are finalized and everyone leaves with a clear understanding of their role and responsibilities for the upcoming program increment.

The energy transitions from intense planning to a sense of readiness and anticipation for the work ahead. Participants leave the event with a clear understanding of their roles and responsibilities, as well as a shared commitment to achieving the goals set forth during the PI Planning event. The leaders are able to achieve this energy curve and outcomes at the event by applying the lean-agile values and mindset.

The Role of the Release Train Engineer (RTE) at PI Planning

The Release Train Engineer (RTE) plays a pivotal role during the PI Planning event. The responsibilities include:

Facilitation: The RTE serves as the primary facilitator of the PI Planning event. They guide the teams through the planning process, ensure adherence to agendas and timeboxes, and facilitate effective communication and collaboration among all participants.

Coordination: RTEs coordinate with various stakeholders, including Product Management, System Architects/Engineering, Scrum Masters, and teams, to align priorities, dependencies, and objectives for the upcoming Program Increment.

Preparation: Prior to the PI Planning event, RTEs work with teams and stakeholders to prepare the necessary artifacts, such as Program Backlogs, Vision and Roadmap, and planning agendas, to ensure a smooth and productive planning session.

Alignment: During the PI Planning event, RTEs ensure that teams align their plans with the overall objectives and priorities of the Agile Release Train (ART) and the organization. They facilitate discussions to resolve conflicts, prioritize features, and make trade-off decisions as needed.

Problem-Solving: RTEs help teams address any impediments, dependencies, or issues that arise during the planning process. They facilitate problem-solving sessions and escalate unresolved issues to appropriate stakeholders for resolution.

Real-Time Adaptation: Throughout the PI Planning event, RTEs remain vigilant for any changes or adjustments needed to the plans. They encourage teams to adapt and iterate their plans in real-time based on new information, feedback, or insights that emerge during the planning session.

Post-Event Follow-Up: After the PI Planning event, RTEs continue to support teams in refining and finalizing their plans. They ensure that teams understand their commitments, dependencies, and objectives for the upcoming Program Increment.

Overall, the RTE's role at the PI Planning event is critical in facilitating collaboration, alignment, and effective planning across the Agile

Release Train, ultimately driving successful execution and delivery of value to customers.

The Role of Product Management at PI Planning

The role of Product Management at PI Planning event is essential for ensuring the successful delivery of value to customers and alignment with business objectives. Here are some key responsibilities and contributions of Product Management during a PI Planning event:

Defining Features and Epics: The Product Manager(s) works closely with the Business Owner and stakeholders to define features and epics that align with the overall business strategy and customer needs. They ensure that the features are prioritized based on business value and customer impact.

Creating the ART Backlog: The Product Manager is responsible for creating and maintaining the ART backlog, which includes features, user stories, and acceptance criteria. They work with the Product Owners and System Architects to slice epics into smaller, actionable features that can be delivered within the PI timeframe.

Collaborating with Agile Teams: During the PI Planning event, the Product Manager collaborates with agile teams to provide guidance, clarification, and context on the features and user stories. They help teams understand the customer requirements and business needs, ensuring that the work is aligned with the product vision.

Participating in Planning Discussions: The Product Manager actively participates in planning discussions to help prioritize features, estimate effort, and identify dependencies. They guide and mentor the teams to create a realistic plan for delivering value to customers during the PI.

Validating Customer Value: Throughout the PI, the Product Manager ensures the validation of PI Objectives. These objectives, crafted by agile teams and demonstrated by Product Owners, are reviewed to ensure they deliver the intended business value to customers. They gather feedback, analyze metrics, and make data-driven decisions to ensure that the product meets customer needs and business expectations.

Adapting to Change: The Product Manager is responsible for adapting to changes in customer requirements, market conditions, and business priorities. They work with teams, through the product owners to adjust the ART backlog and priorities as needed to respond to changing circumstances.

Overall, Product Management plays a critical role in driving product success, ensuring customer satisfaction, and maximizing business value during a PI Planning event. By collaborating with stakeholders, product owners and system architects, guiding the agile teams, and prioritizing work based on customer needs, they contribute to the effective delivery of value and the achievement of business objectives.

The Role of System Architect / Engineering at PI Planning

The role of System Architects/Engineering during the PI Planning event is pivotal in ensuring the technical feasibility and coherence of the planned features and initiatives across the ART. Their role includes:

Technical Leadership: System Architects/Engineering provide technical leadership and expertise during the planning event. They help teams understand the technical implications of their planned work and guide them in making informed decisions.

Architecture Vision: They contribute to defining and communicating the architecture vision for the upcoming PI. This includes aligning the technical direction with the overall business goals and objectives. They ensure that the architecture and design of the system align with the overall technical vision and principles established for the enterprise. They provide guidance on architectural patterns, standards, and best practices to ensure consistency and scalability.

Dependency Management: System Architects/Engineering identify and manage dependencies between teams and components within the system. They work with teams to resolve dependencies and mitigate risks that may impact the successful delivery of the planned features and capabilities.

Risk Management: They assess technical risks associated with the planned work and collaborate with teams to develop mitigation strategies. They anticipate potential challenges and help teams proactively address them to minimize disruptions during the PI.

Integration Planning: System architects/engineering collaborate with teams to plan for the integration of new features or changes into the existing system architecture. They help identify integration points, APIs, data flows, and interfaces required for seamless integration.

Quality Assurance: System Architects/Engineering collaborate with teams to ensure that the planned work meets quality standards and guidelines. They participate in discussions about testing strategies, and non-functional requirements to ensure a high-quality outcome.

Performance Optimization: They assist teams in optimizing system performance and scalability considerations during the planning process. This may involve identifying performance bottlenecks, tuning configurations, and recommending performance improvement strategies.

Technical Debt Management: System architects/engineering help teams identify and address technical debt accrued during previous PIs or as legacy delivery. They provide guidance on prioritizing and mitigating technical debt while balancing it with new feature development.

Overall, System Architects/Engineering play a crucial role in aligning technical direction with business objectives, mitigating technical risks, and ensuring the technical integrity of the planned work during the PI Planning event, enabling teams to deliver high-quality, scalable, and maintainable solutions that align with the organization's strategic objectives. Their involvement helps foster collaboration and coherence across Agile Release Trains, ultimately contributing to the successful delivery of value to the customer.

The Role of the Business Owner at PI Planning

The role of a Business Owner at the PI Planning event is crucial to the success of the planning process and the overall alignment of business objectives with the executing agile teams of the ART. Here are some key responsibilities and contributions of a Business Owner during a PI Planning event:

Setting Strategic Direction: The Business Owner is responsible for providing strategic direction and priorities to the ART. They communicate the business goals, vision, and objectives that need to be achieved during the PI.

Prioritizing Features and Epics: The Business Owner works closely with the Product Management team to prioritize features and epics based on business value and strategic importance. They help in making decisions on what should be included in the PI based on the overall business strategy.

Participating in Planning Discussions: The Business Owner actively participates in planning discussions during the PI Planning event. They provide guidance, clarification, and context to the teams on the business requirements and expectations.

Resolving Dependencies: Business Owners help identify and resolve cross-team dependencies that may impact on the successful delivery of features during the PI. They collaborate with other Business Owners and stakeholders to ensure alignment and coordination across teams. This can be part of the Management problem Solving session within the PI Planning as well as across the rest of the event.

Approving the PI Objectives: The Business Owner reviews the PI Objectives that are set by the agile teams and ensures that the PI Objectives align with the overall business goals and deliver acceptable business value within the PI timeframe. This is reflected by a planned business value (BV) score on a linear scale of 1-10, 1 being the least business value acceptable and 10 being the highest.

Monitoring Progress: During the PI, the Business Owner oversees the advancement of PI Objectives and evaluates the attainment of business outcomes. They offer feedback and guidance to the teams, ensuring their alignment with business priorities during their involvement in the ART System Demos and Portfolio Syncs.

Overall, the Business Owner plays a critical role in bridging the gap between business strategy and ART execution during a PI Planning event. By actively engaging with the teams, providing strategic direction, and ensuring alignment with business goals, they contribute to the success of the PI and the overall business agility of the organization.

How Did You Fix a PI Planning Event that Went Bad?

By Bonsy Yelsangi, CST

I was invited to observe a PI Planning session and within first 15 minutes I knew it was not going to be a productive session because of the below observations:

- 2 SMEs (Subject Matter Experts) that were crucial to the planning were not available to attend the meeting since they were not invited well in advance.

- The Product Backlog items were not refined in advance by the Product Owners.

- There were too many open questions which were not answered, leading to confusion about the commitment from the team.

- The past activity of the teams was not being taken into consideration for planning.

My suggestion was to cut short the planning session, take the rest of the day to get all the ducks in a row, and resume the session the following day. In the remaining half of the day, we did the following:

- We requested that those 2 missing SMEs spend time reviewing the Product Backlog and attend at least half of the PI Planning session the following day. We assured them that we would give ample time to plan and adjust their calendars before the next PI Planning session began.

- The Product Owner (armed with all the questions from the Developers) collaborated with stakeholders and tried to get as much information as possible.

- The Developers were encouraged to collaborate with the Product Owner to refine their PBIs.

Conversely, Any Example of a PI Planning Event that Went Great, and What Helped It?

By Bonsy Yelsangi, CST

The most important factor in a successful PI Planning event is the planning and preparation done before the event begins. As a Scrum Master, one must work with Product Owners and Developers to ensure that they are thoroughly prepared with their set of tasks. I would always prepare checklists to help them stay focused and organized.

Also, SMs must ensure that teams have time to reflect on the previous Sprints and what improvements they will be implementing in the following Sprints.

Executing a smooth planning process takes preparation, alignment, and communication.

Questions and Answers about PI Planning

Question: *"What Is the Best Way to Estimate User Stories?"*

For the teams to plan their Sprints during PI Planning, they need to have estimates for the work items or for Stories in their Team Backlog. Otherwise, it is impossible to know how much work they can put into a Sprint. So, they need to spend some time refining the work items and estimating the work. Once they have the estimates for each work item or Story, they can compare those estimates to the team's Velocity and decide how many of these work items the team can commit to doing in each Sprint.

Many teams estimate using story points.

"What are story points?"

They are numbers that reflect the relative size of a work item or a Story compared to the size of a baseline Story. The baseline Story is typically a small Story and it is set at 1 point. If a Story has the same size of the baseline, then its estimate is 1 point. If a Story has a size that is double the baseline, its estimate is 2 points. If a Story has a size that is 8 eight times the size of the baseline, then its estimate is 8 points. And so on.

The size of a Story is estimated based on the amount of effort required to complete the work on that Story.

"What is effort?"

It is a combination of the amount of work, the complexity of the work, the level of knowledge of the team, and any uncertainty on doing the work. Notice that the size is not based on time (the time we "think" it will take to complete it). We prefer to base estimates on the level of effort, and not on the time that we think is necessary for its completion.

108

Knowing that estimates are never exact or accurate (in fact, estimates are always "wrong" because they are only estimates), the goal is never to, say,

"Oh, let us spend a lot of time here so we can really come down to the nitty-gritty details, and make sure that the estimate is the right one."

That is often a waste of time, because it is never going to happen that you get the "right" estimate anyway.

So, you want to spend some time having a discussion with the team and to understand the work. Get enough understanding to be on the same page, and then to estimate the work item. Leave yourself a little wiggle room in those estimates to make sure that you can deliver the work even when the estimate is not correct (you should account for any uncertainty or complexity).

A good practice is to have a buffer on capacity. Every Sprint, at Sprint Planning, you should leave a little bit of capacity that you do not use for your plan. That buffer is going to compensate for any uncertainty on the work, any complexity that you cannot predict, or any estimates that may not be accurate. A good practice is to establish an initial buffer of 10% to 20% of your Velocity. Some teams may need a larger buffer if they need to cover for a lot of unexpected work requests that may show up in the middle of the Sprint.

A side note: some teams may use a "no-estimate" approach, that is, they do not estimate the individual work items or Stories. They do not use story points, or T-shirt sizing. They just do not estimate the work items. Even these teams need to establish capacity for each Sprint and decide how many work items or Stories they can commit to doing in each Sprint. They do this by calculating Velocity based on the number of work items or number of Stories completed in prior Sprints.

Regardless of the specific estimation approach or technique your team uses, the goal of estimation is to be able to decide how much work your team can commit to doing in each Sprint, so that it fits within the available capacity, and it is not based on some unattainable stretch objective, or wild dream. So, do not stress too much about the estimates, and instead focus on establishing a commitment for each Sprint that is attainable.

Question: *"Do We Wait Until PI Planning to Estimate the Stories for the PI?"*

There is a lot of work for the teams to do at PI Planning, including prioritizing the work, identifying dependencies, creating PI Objectives, and discussing risks. Waiting to do refinement and estimation at PI Planning for every Story that the team is responsible for, may actually be too much work in the limited time available at PI Planning.

A good practice is to do a level of refinement before PI Planning. This gives everyone on the team an idea of what the upcoming work is, what the priorities are, how to break down the work into smaller Stories, and how much effort is required for each Story. It may even allow your team to start discussing any dependencies with other teams, further helping to set expectations ahead of PI Planning.

Notice that this is not intended to replace the refinement work that you need to do at PI Planning. That still needs to happen. Those work items and those priorities may even change before the day of PI Planning, so nothing should really be set in stone. But, if you do this, you can get part of the work started earlier so you do not have to do the whole thing at PI Planning.

PI Planning becomes that pivotal moment where all of the plans from different teams come together, get aligned, and are finalized.

Question: *"How Should Product Management Collaborate with Product Owners?"*

Consider what happens when work requests flow top-down from Product Management to the Product Owners.

This one-way stream creates a lot of problems, including lack of context, disempowerment of the Product Owners, unattainable objectives imposed on the Agile Teams, and lack of clarity on priorities (or continuously changing priorities).

> Product Management and Product Owners should constantly collaborate with each other. Yes, they have responsibilities at different levels, but they all are accountable for building the right product for their customers.

Therefore, the flow of work should be a two-way stream:

- **Product Management** establishes the overall vision, roadmap, and priorities (at higher levels) for the product based on business and customer needs. They then share these with the Product Owners.
- **Product Owners** refine the vision, the roadmap, and the priorities based on their understanding of the customer needs, the capacity of their teams, and any new ideas they may offer. They then push back with Product Management and create alignment of what actually can be done and what can be achieved.

If you establish this two-way work stream and collaboration between Product Management and the Product Owners, refinement is continuous. It does not happen all at once at PI Planning, but instead, Product Owners are involved in the decisions, the design, and the priorities affecting the product. And when the time comes for PI Planning, the Product Owners are better equipped to provide context and guide the teams in decision-making.

At a minimum, this collaboration should happen at the PO Sync event, which is a weekly meeting between Product Management and the Product Owners to sync on vision, roadmap, priorities, and objectives. Of course, the more you create an environment of collaboration and transparency (rather than an opposite environment of hierarchy and top-down decision-making) the more everyone is going to be empowered, motivated, and informed on product decisions. And this will, in turn, allow your teams to create better products.

Question: *"How Do We Estimate a Dependency from Another Team?"*

"What if we get a dependency from somebody else on another team? How do we know how much work there is to do? How do we decide when to schedule the work?"

Supporting dependencies from other teams – while planning your own work - is a challenge. And sometimes, these dependencies are shared with you only at the last minute, maybe after you already have figured out your own plan, and now you need to consider the additional work that is required to support that dependency.

To understand the effect of supporting that dependency on your own team, you may need to come up with an estimate.

"How much work is there to do? What is the complexity? What is the level of effort? Will this fit within our capacity, or do we need to change our plan?"

Understanding the level of effort required for a dependency means that you must spend a little bit of time opening the work item and understanding what it is that you need to do. Sometimes, you need to call the other team and say,

"Can you come over here and please explain what it is that we need to do for you?"

Let us be on the same page.

Yes, it may require some refinement work to really understand what is required to support that dependency, and your team may need some time to come up with an estimate. You may even need to break up a large work item into smaller Stories if the estimate is too large for a Sprint.

My suggestion is, invite someone from the other team (the one who depends on your team) when you do refinement of your Team Backlog. This will go a long way toward creating a shared understanding of that dependency and aligning the work between the two teams.

Question: *"Do We Need to Plan Every Story Given to Us for a PI?"*

The short answer is no. The goal of PI Planning is not for your team to cram as many Stories as possible into a PI, and especially not to cram all of the work given to you by Product Management, just because they "say so."

Remember, it should be a two-way collaboration between Product Management and the Product Owners. Yes, the job of Product Management is to give the teams enough work to keep them productive, and very likely that means pushing them to deliver more.

But this should not be a top-down directive. You may end up exerting excessive pressure on the teams, multitasking, lowering the quality of the work due to shortcuts or compromises, and accumulating technical debt.

Instead, establish an environment where Product Owners collaborate with Product Management on what is attainable, and what is not. Align on what the key priorities are for everyone, and what is nice to have but lower in priority.

At PI Planning, Product Management provides a list of Features to the teams to work on. It is the responsibility of each team to create a plan that is attainable. If the Features are too large, too complex, or too many, the teams should push back and declare what can be attainable in the PI, and what cannot be. The keywords here are transparency, collaboration, and commitment.

There is no value for a team to establish a plan that is too bold or too unattainable, and then to commit to deliver it. This approach will result in negative behaviors.

Instead, guide the Team Members to commit to a plan that they know they can deliver 100%. That means committing to an attainable plan that fits within capacity. The expectation should be that the team delivers 100% of its plan by the end of the Sprint.

And, in case a team does not complete 100% of its commitment, do not penalize the team. Instead, have a conversation at Retrospective and discuss what the team can improve in its planning process to establish more predictable plans. The team's predictability measure can be helpful in driving this conversation (Predictability measure = Total work completed / Total work planned)[xviii].

Empower Product Thinking in SAFe

Outputs vs. Outcomes

In product development, it is important to draw distinctions between outputs (building a series of features or releasing a product in the market), and outcomes (delivering value to your customers and to your business).

An **output** is what you produce as a result of your organization's activities. Outputs include new features and functionalities, bug fixes, and product releases. Measures of output are based on the quantity of work completed, rather than on the value or on the impact of your services for your clients. These metrics tend to become vanity metrics: improvements in these metrics do not necessarily lead to an increase in customer or in business value. For example, you will measure how many new features you launched in a month, or how frequently you release updates for your product. While these are important, they may not represent value: you could launch a ton of new features, but if your customers do not use them, you have created no value.

An **outcome** is a measurable result that your product or service delivers to your customers and to your business. An outcome is measured in terms of the value delivered, or on behavior change. It is grounded in solving needs and in creating opportunities. For example, a new e-commerce website with better descriptions and search, has helped customers find clothing that matches their style and their sustainability preferences. Customers are satisfied (customer outcome), and they return for more sustainable products (behavior change that leads to a business outcome).

Outcomes are usually measured with value metrics.

The Two Types of Outcomes

There are two types of outcomes that Product Managers focus on:

Customer outcomes: These represent the value that your product or your service delivers for your customers.

Business outcomes: These represent the value that your product or your service generates for your business.

Notice that business value is secondary to the customer value: if you do not deliver value to your customers or to your end users, you will not generate much value for your business. However, business outcomes are equally important as you will not be in business for long if your product activities do not generate value. Therefore, Product Managers should understand and deliver both customer and business outcomes with their product.

Product Managers build products to generate outcomes. Outputs without outcomes are useless expenses of efforts and resources. Therefore, the job of the Product Managers is to first understand what outcomes we need to deliver (to customers and to the business), and then to decide the specific activities that we need to accomplish in order to generate those outcomes.

Why Product Managers/Owners Exist

The end goal of a product is to serve its customers (or end users) and to deliver value. This translates into the main responsibility of Product Managers and Product Owners (POs). Product Managers and Product Owners are accountable for maximizing the value delivered by their product: They exist to serve their customers, to understand how to deliver outcomes, and to build great products that deliver value.[xix]

Yet, too often, in a hierarchical organization, the Product Owners exist to serve the Product Managers, and Product Managers exist to serve their leadership. Product decisions are made at the top, execution priorities trickle down the chain, and the Agile Teams become *delivery teams*: their main responsibility becomes the delivery of work. Teams are no longer measured on the value delivered, but rather on the amount of work produced.

When building new products, the work is typically complex, accounting for multiple components and moving parts, uncertainty, and ambiguity. When building products for new customers, for new markets, or that use a new technology, there are a lot of items that need to be discovered, tested, and validated.

That is why Product Managers and Product Owners exist. Not to drive delivery of the work (although they need to do this too), but to figure out if the product idea makes sense, if the market is going to accept it, if we can build it, and if the customers care about it. They are responsible for answering these questions about the product:

> **Feasible:** Can we build it in an effective and cost-effective manner?
>
> **Usable:** Do customers use it and enjoy doing so?
>
> **Valuable:** Does the product deliver value and satisfy customer needs?
>
> **Viable:** Can we build it in a way that delivers outcomes to the business (e.g., can we make money)?

Empowered product teams have the freedom to research, to analyze data, and to make informed decisions about the product roadmap and the feature development. They are trusted to identify the best course of action based on their expertise and understanding of the market.

While empowered teams have autonomy, they are also held accountable for the success (or failure) of their decisions and for the outcomes delivered. This fosters a sense of ownership and motivates them to deliver results.

Why Is Value Important and What Is Value Based On?

By Jason Tanner, CST and Luke Hohmann, SAFe Fellow

We define value as the **benefits a customer receives minus the total cost of ownership**. We identify and quantify value based on the tangible and intangible benefits a software-enabled solution provides to customers. Perception of value drives the pricing and monetization mode, which drives the economic sustainability of the solution. Economic sustainability is the prerequisite for solution sustainability, the ability to deliver value to customers over time.

Value cannot be nebulous. Product Managers, including Product Owners, bear the responsibility to deeply understand customer needs to determine the value of their solution.

Adopting a Product Thinking Mindset

If the goal of a product is to deliver outcomes that customers value, it is necessary to start any work from understanding what objectives we want to achieve with the solution. We should define the objectives first, and then figure out the best solution to deliver these objectives.

Compare the two approaches in the picture.

TOP-DOWN APPROACH

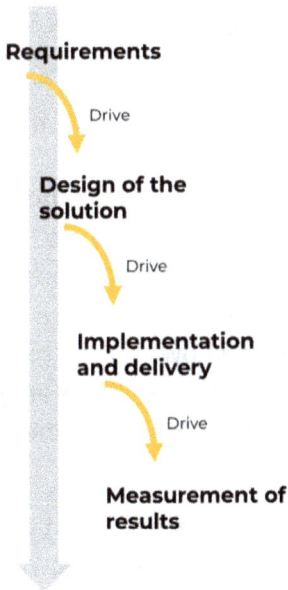

Requirements

Drive

Design of the solution

Drive

Implementation and delivery

Drive

Measurement of results

Result is output.
All risk is at the end.
Results are measured after delivery.

PRODUCT THINKING APPROACH

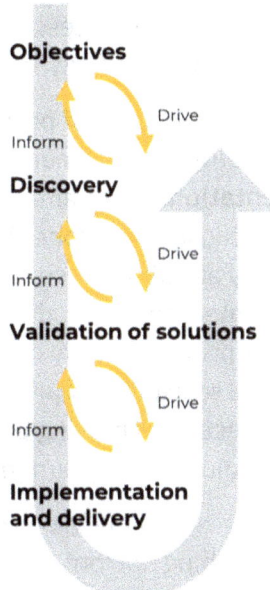

Objectives

Drive
Inform

Discovery

Drive
Inform

Validation of solutions

Drive
Inform

Implementation and delivery

Result are outcomes.
Risk is mitigated at each step.
Outcomes are measured throughout.

Top-down Approach

In a traditional, top-down approach, requirements are defined first and they drive the solution. Often, the requirements, and sometimes even the solutions, are given by the customers and by the stakeholders at the beginning of a new project. The product team is tasked with the implementation and the delivery of the solutions, as requested.

In this approach, results are measured at the end, when the solutions are built and the feedback (or metrics) are evaluated. The risk is all at the end: we do not know if we have built the right solution until we measure the performance of the product or collect feedback about its use from the customers. With high risk, comes high cost: if anything is off, it may be costly to go back and to change it.

The product development team may break the work into smaller chunks and may deliver each increment in a Sprint. While this incremental delivery is better than an all-at-once delivery of the solution, the work still follows a top-down approach in which the actual results are measured once the full solution is delivered.

This approach is not necessarily bad. In some situations, it may be effective and straightforward.

These typically consist of **projects that are well defined in scope, in understanding of customer needs**, and **in know-how of the implementation.** The team knows how to build the correct solution (maybe because it has done similar work before) and there is little uncertainty about the customer needs and the requirements. Work is clearly defined, so the product development team can just execute it. Even if the project is fairly complicated,[xx] the team knows how to break it down and to execute it properly based on its experience. There are multiple pieces and moving parts, but there is little uncertainty. The expected solution is well understood.

But not all projects fall in this category. In fact, we often think that we know everything upfront, when in reality, there are a lot of unknowns that we are unaware of.

Product Thinking Approach

Building a new product is usually a complex endeavor. The customer may be new, the target market may be new, the requirements may be unclear, or the team may not have prior experience in building something similar. We could be making assumptions about the solution, about the customer needs, or about our ability to satisfy what customers need in an effective and viable way. If any of these assumptions prove wrong, we may end up with a solution that nobody wants.

Building a new product is typically a risky endeavor. We cannot wait to measure results after we have built the full product, because at that point, *les jeux sont fait*: the product is built, and if we missed the mark, any change is going to be expensive.

We need a different approach.

What if we started with objectives?

Rather than defining a set of requirements, we can define a set of objectives. This helps to clarify and to focus on the key outcomes that our solution should deliver, for example, what customer problem we should solve, or what new opportunity we should create.

Then, discovery activities help us define the problem better, and possibly to ideate solutions. We may not know (yet) which solution is the best, and we spend time in validation. We could build a prototype or an MVP (Minimum Viable Product) of the solution, test it with customers, and get their feedback. Then, we could decide whether the solution works (and we should continue building it), or if we should think about something different.

Notice that the feedback loop is built in, in this approach: work is not top-down, but rather is iterative. Learning from each activity may inform decisions made at a prior point. Every time we learn something more, we may revisit the assumptions we have made at a prior step, redefine the solution, and validate something new.

This process continues until we collect enough evidence (with metrics measured or feedback from customers) that confirms that the solution is worth building. The implementation now follows a much lower risk profile because measurements happen throughout the development process and not all at the end.

This is a product thinking approach.

The Product Thinking Mindset

Many SAFe practices allow teams to build a product faster, but how do we know if we are building the **right product**?

Infusing an effective product thinking mindset is key to the success of a product initiative and to a SAFe implementation.[xxi] Therefore, I always spend as much time working with product teams and their leadership in adopting the right product practices, as I spend on SAFe practices.

While SAFe supports both approaches, a top-down approach should be employed only for clearly defined projects. Other than those, organizations should strive to adopt a product thinking approach and empower the Product Managers and the Product Owners to own product decisions (and outcomes delivered), collaborate, and establish a feedback loop to influence broader product decisions made at the top.

Product thinking is essentially a problem-solving approach to creating products. It focuses on understanding the needs of users, the goals of the business, and the limitations and the possibilities of technology to develop successful products.

A product thinking mindset:

- Focuses on understanding user needs and on solving real problems.

- Prioritizes creating value and delivering outcomes to both customers and to the business.

- Starts from clearly defining the target outcomes and then works backward to define what to build to achieve these outcomes.

- Emphasizes experimentation, iteration, and data-driven decision making, rather than upfront static planning.

- Builds products that deliver an engaging customer experience, that provide high satisfaction, and that drive customer retention.

- Adapts to changing market conditions, quickly testing new ideas, and updating plans as needed.

- Empowers product teams to own product decisions, to adapt to customer feedback, and to influence product decisions.

How to Spark Product Thinking in SAFe

SAFe emphasizes planning and predictability, which can be great for large enterprises. However, to truly deliver impactful products, it is important to integrate a product-thinking approach into the product development process. Here are some ways for Product Managers and Product Owners to spark product thinking within SAFe:

Align on PI Objectives: Do not relegate PI Objectives to the "*it is just another process to follow*" bin. Instead, leverage the PI Objectives and use them to create transparency and alignment on key outcomes. Make sure that the members of the Agile Team know them. For example, remind the objectives at each Sprint Planning, and revisit them at Sprint Review and at System Demo.

Embrace customer centricity: SAFe already emphasizes customer centricity. Capitalize on this by ensuring deep customer understanding that informs all decision making throughout the PI. For example, define the PI Objectives in terms of customer outcomes, not in terms of Features to deliver.

Move beyond Features: Do not just build Features; focus on solving customer problems and on delivering outcomes. This considers the entire user experience, from initial setup to ongoing interaction. Instead of defining Features as a list of requirements, define Features as the key outcome you would like to deliver to your customers. SAFe offers a framework for doing this with the Benefit Hypothesis.

Focus on value streams: Structure the Agile Release Train (ART) around value streams. This ensures that teams are constantly focused on delivering value to customers, rather than just completing Features. ARTs can also evolve over time, to align better with evolving value streams. Product Managers should understand the value stream they are supporting, with a focus on the Customer Value Stream (more on this later).

Support continuous learning: Encourage a culture of experimentation and learning throughout the development process. Allow for course correction based on customer feedback and on market changes. Leverage the Sprint Review and the System Demo to actually learn from your stakeholders and from customers, and not just to do a PowerPoint presentation about your work.

Craft a compelling vision: Create and share the product vision with both the stakeholders and the members of the Agile Teams. Regularly communicate the product vision and its connection to user needs. Craft a compelling product vision that outlines the desired future state and excites the team. A compelling vision creates alignment around a common goal, sparks a sense of purpose in achieving it, and defines focus for everyone involved in the product development effort. Having a clear sense of purpose is a key lever of motivation for the team.[xxii]

Challenge the hypotheses behind product Epics and Features: Epics and Features define large functionalities to implement into the product. Their goal should be to solve a problem, to create an opportunity, or to address a need. They should deliver a clear outcome to the customers and to the business. If you are not clear about the intended outcome, or about what problem the Epic/Feature intends to solve, challenge the underlying hypotheses. Do your discovery and validation activities. Before building the full functionality, build a prototype and test it with your customers. Make sure there is alignment between the functionality you are going to build, and the outcome you intend to deliver.

Prioritize experiments: Allocate time and resources for testing product hypotheses. Encourage the Agile Team members to experiment with different ideas and approaches. Empower the Product Owners to decide which experiments to run and what to build to validate the hypotheses. Share the results from these experiments to help the product team make decisions on what to do next.

Leverage the Developers' expertise: When you define User Stories, leave space for the Developers to identify the best solution for implementation, rather than fixing all the details upfront. User Stories should define who the user is, what they need, and why they need it (the outcome they expect to get from it). The details about the solution can be left to the Developers.

Become a product thought leader: Stay informed and continuously learn about product management trends, user research methods, and design thinking principles. Learn and practice techniques to adopt product thinking within SAFe (I acknowledge you for reading this book!). Educate and inspire the product community of practice on product thinking. Share resources and lead discussions on user-centric design and product strategy.

Collaborate: Foster collaboration between the Product Owners, the Product Managers, and the Epic Owners to share progress on the objectives, to clarify outcomes, and to influence product decisions. The PO Sync should act as a feedback loop and not as a one-way stream of top-down directives.

Empowered Product Teams

In the fast-moving culture of Silicon Valley's startups, empowered product teams are cross-functional groups of individuals who are not just tasked with building products, but who are also given the ownership and authority to define the product vision, to solve customer problems, and to make strategic decisions throughout the development life cycle. This stands in contrast to traditional models where product development teams might simply execute on a predefined roadmap dictated by leadership.

While every product organization strives to emulate the structure of Silicon Valley's best companies, their model is often aspirational and may not fit most organizational structures directly.

For example, in a sales-led organization, the sales team represents the key stakeholders. Product Managers may receive requests for new functionalities from the sales team. These requests are expected to be satisfied and to be delivered to customers as soon as possible. Product Managers may have limited space to ideate or to experiment with alternative solutions or to push back against a new request that does not fit with their product vision.

When scaling Agile from a few teams to dozens of teams, the complexity of building a large product and of decision making, multiplies. When implementing a scaled approach, it is important to consider the context of the organization, its culture, and its organizational model. Trying to impose a predefined model or a model from another organization, may lead to failure. There are plenty of examples of companies that tried to adopt the Spotify model and failed to grow.

But even within the constraints of an organization's model and culture, product teams should strive to adopt a product thinking mindset.

Product thinking should be considered a strategic approach to driving product success in today's dynamic market. By fostering a culture of ownership, autonomy, and accountability, companies can unlock the full potential of their teams and deliver products that truly delight their customers.

The Empowered Epic Owner

The main responsibility of an Epic Owner is to shepherd Epics through the initial stages of discovery, analysis, and refinement, all the way to the implementation and to the delivery of a new functionality. The Epic Owner uses a Kanban board at the Portfolio level to visualize the different stages of an Epic and to keep track of its status.

The problem with Epics is that they represent large bodies of work that could take multiple months, sometimes quarters, to complete. Sometimes Epics are fully scoped, all requirements and implementation details defined, and approvals gathered, before they are executed. Treating an Epic as a monolithic work item and expecting to build the whole thing, can lead to a waste of resources and time.

> *"The best way to get a good idea is to get a lot of ideas."*
>
> James Webb Young

This quote emphasizes the value of diverse perspectives and can be interpreted to support empowering those closest to the work to contribute ideas and make decisions. Epic Owners should collaborate closely with Product Managers and Product Owners to inform decisions on the Epics, to define an MVP, and to validate outcomes.

An empowered Epic Owner:

- The Epic Owner should be more than a "shepherd" who tracks the status of each Epic. The Epic Owner should adopt product thinking and validate expectations behind an Epic before full commitment.

- Epic Owners can define an MVP and work with Product Managers to define MVFs (Minimum Viable Features). Rather than scoping out the full specs of an Epic, identify the critical components, and work with the product team to define the minimum version of those components that could help to validate if the Epic itself is valuable, and to decide whether to continue building the rest of the Epic, or pivot to a different solution.

The Empowered Product Manager

Product Managers own and refine the ART Backlog which defines a prioritized list of Features that need to be completed in order to deliver the Epic. The Product Managers break the Epic into Features, and then prioritize Features for implementation by the ART.

However, when Features are fully scoped with a list of requirements and implementation details about the solution, the Agile Teams become delivery teams: they are the receiving end of work directives that specify what to do and how to do it.

Monolithic Features can lead to a waste of time and resources. They can also lead to bloated products, with tons of Features that are not needed or used by customers. When Epics get broken into monolithic Features, the Epic itself becomes harder and bigger to build, causing additional delays and wasted effort.

Product Managers should be empowered to:

- Identify the **key Features** to build in order to deliver the expected value, and to **validate** if the overall Epic makes sense.

- By adopting a product thinking approach, Product Managers should clearly define the problem that they are trying to solve, and then validate possible solutions.

- Instead of defining Features in terms of what the Feature will do (with detailed specifications of the HOW the Features should be implemented), they should define the Features in terms of **what problem they solve for the customer,** or what they help the customer achieve. A Feature should clearly specify the outcomes it helps deliver (shift the focus from the HOW to the WHY).

- Specify a Feature as the **problem-to-solve** and as a **hypothesis statement** about the solution, rather than as a predetermined list of specifications.

The Empowered Product Owner

Agile Teams are often considered delivery teams: they are responsible for delivering a solution given to them by Product Management. This leaves little space for ideation, innovation, or adaptation. And it can lead to a waste of resources and bloated products.

Rather than assigning Features to Agile Teams with predefined specifications and implementation details (treating the Agile Team as a delivery machine), specify the problem-to-solve and the hypothesis to validate. Then, let the Product Owner and the Agile Team figure out the best way to implement the Feature. By doing this, you create agency with the Product Owners, and allow the Agile Team to experiment with possible solutions, driving innovation, and possibly addressing the customer need in a more effective way.

> *"Empowerment is giving people the authority to make decisions and take ownership of their work."*
>
> Stephen Covey

Empowered Product Owners:

- **Own the HOW**: they can define, experiment with, and validate the best way to implement a Feature.

- **Are clear about the WHY**: If the problem that a Feature is trying to solve is not clear, the solution cannot be effective.

Empowered Product Owners understand the value of building a Feature and the outcomes that are expected from it.

- **Measure the outcomes**: A *delivery team* builds a solution, but is not responsible if the solution is not effective (it was given to them by someone else). Instead, an empowered Product Owner measures the effectiveness of the solution they have built and determines if the solution delivers the expected outcomes.

- **Influence product decisions**: While work requests flow from Epics, to Features, to Stories, feedback about what worked and what did not, and the outcomes delivered, should flow backward. This feedback loop helps everyone on the product team (Epic Owners, Product Managers, and Product Owners) understand the impact of the work they are doing, and whether alternative solutions should be explored.

The Problem with Feature Factories

A *feature factory* is a term used to describe a company structure or a mindset where the focus is on churning out Features for a product or a service, often at the expense of quality or customer value.

When teams behave like feature factories, they churn out widgets at an ever-increasing rate, giving a false sense of accomplishment. Several problems may generate from the never-ending flow of outputs:

Frustrated users: Products become overloaded with features that users do not need or understand, leading to a poor user experience.

Slow or lack of response to change: Plans and roadmaps are defined upfront. Work is broken down and assigned to teams for delivery. When changes are required, the teams are already overloaded with work, and cannot adapt quickly.

Demotivation and burnout: Development teams that are constantly under pressure to deliver new features, can become disengaged and burned out.

Wasted resources: Time and effort are spent building features that ultimately do not provide value, leading to inefficiency, waste, and higher costs.

Decreased innovation: The focus on churning out features can stifle innovation and the exploration of new ideas. Teams are pressured to increase productivity (measured by outputs) and are not given the space or flexibility to research new ideas or to drive innovation.

Avoid Feature Factories

When you scale from one team to multiple teams, or introduce organizational levels to manage the complexity of a product, it is easy to lose agility. Product decisions are made at the top and then distributed to the lower levels for execution. Given the scale of the organization, dozens of features may be developed at a given time. Teams may focus on churning outputs, rather than on producing outcomes.

SAFe itself is not inherently designed to create feature factories, but certain ways of implementing SAFe can lead to those characteristics. Typically, these problems stem from an organization used to a top-down product planning approach and from a lack of a truly agile mindset: when the organization adopts SAFe, it is easier to maintain the traditional approach rather than transforming it.

Here are a few examples of how SAFe implementations can turn into feature factories:

Product decisions flow top-to-bottom: Epics get prioritized and then broken down into Features and into Stories. The Agile Teams are pressured to deliver ever more Stories. There is no feedback loop from the Agile Teams back to the Epic level to determine if the work is valuable or to validate if the solution delivers outcomes.

Overly granular backlogs: SAFe emphasizes breaking down work into smaller, manageable Stories. While this can be helpful, overly granular backlogs can lead to teams focusing on churning out small features, becoming slow in reacting to change, and having difficulties properly prioritizing valuable work.

Misinterpretation of value streams: SAFe leverages the concept of value streams to break down the flow of work and to distribute it among multiple teams. However, sometimes teams focus solely on delivering their part of the value stream without considering the overall product strategy or how their contribution integrates with other teams to deliver value to the customers.

Lack of focus on outcomes: SAFe promotes iteration and delivery, but there is a risk of prioritizing feature delivery over measuring outcomes. If teams are not measuring customer outcomes, or business impact, they might fall into the trap of building features that do not solve real problems.

Disconnect between teams and business strategy: The various levels of SAFe can create a division between feature teams and the overall business strategy. If teams are not aligned with the bigger picture and user needs, they might build features that do not contribute to the product's long-term goals.

From Feature Factory to Empowered Teams

Moving from feature factories to empowered teams requires a shift in mindset, structure, and processes.

> *"Innovation thrives in an environment where the people closest to the customers and to the technology have the authority to experiment and make decisions."*
>
> Carly Fiorina

Here is a roadmap to guide you through the transition:

Define Success and Empower Ownership

Shift focus from features to outcomes: Empowered teams own the success of a product area, not just delivering features. Define objectives and clear metrics that measure customer value and business impact, not just output like the number of features shipped.

Empower decision making: Give teams the authority to make decisions about product direction, prioritization, and roadmaps. Encourage experimentation and calculated risks.

Create feedback loops: Avoid top-down decision making and instead create feedback loops from the Agile Teams that are building the product back to the higher-level decision makers. Limit structures and hierarchies, and instead create collaboration and transparency among Product Owners, Product Managers, and Epic Owners using PO Sync meetings.

Define clear product vision and strategy: Have a clear roadmap and understand how each feature contributes to the overall product goals. Develop objective-based roadmaps that are based on outcomes rather than on outputs.

Focus on user needs: Prioritize features that solve real problems and that deliver value to users. Conduct user research and validate ideas before development. Use Discovery activities, prototypes, and MVPs to learn and to decide what is valuable and important.

Build Cross-functional Teams

Assemble diverse skillsets: Do not silo teams by functional area or by component. Empowered teams should be cross-functional, with members who possess a range of skills needed to bring a full Feature or product to life.

Shared ownership and accountability: Everyone on the team feels responsible for the product's success, not just their individual tasks. This fosters collaboration and a sense of ownership.

Empower the Agile Team: Product Owners, Designers, and Developers partner on product decision-making and collaborate to define the feature's usability, feasibility, and viability.

Foster a Culture of Learning and Experimentation

Embrace the Third Way of DevOps: Encourage trying new things, learning from failures, and adapting to changing environments. Do not penalize taking (small) risks and failing. Leverage the learning opportunity and enable sharing across all teams or the organization.

Invest in continuous learning: Provide opportunities for team members to develop new skills and to stay up-to-date on industry trends. Create space for innovation, using capacity allocation, IP Sprints, or by organizing hackathons. Engage Developers in Discovery and validation activities with customers.

Validate ideas before committing: Before committing to a solution, a new feature, or an entire Epic, find a way to experiment, to test, and to validate the idea. Build an MVP (Minimum Viable Product) or an MVF (Minimum Viable Feature) and test it. If it does not deliver value, pivot quickly. Do this before committing to a full development.

Invest in collaboration tools: Utilize tools that facilitate communication, information sharing, and real-time visibility into progress. Track progress on objectives, not on output completed.

Lead by Example and Provide Support

Leadership buy-in: Leadership needs to champion this shift and to provide resources to empower teams.

Coaching and mentorship: Offers guidance and support to help teams navigate the transition.

Celebrate successes: Recognizes and rewards teams for demonstrating empowered behaviors and for achieving positive outcomes.

Managing Epics and MVPs

Epics and Refinement of Epics

When you start a new project or a new initiative, you typically start with some bold ideas. Maybe there are some major functionalities that you want to build into your product. These are large bodies of work, and we call them Epics.

"What is an Epic?"

An Epic is a major work item, something that we need to do, and it may take a significant effort to complete. Think about a major functionality in your system, or a full redesign of the UI (User Interface) of a website. Typically, we spend multiple months, sometimes even multiple quarters, on these Epics, because they are really quite large.

Because of their size, there is no way for an Agile Team to take an Epic and to complete it within a Sprint. So, in order for the teams to execute the work, they need to take an Epic and to split it into smaller work items. To follow the SAFe hierarchy, you can split Epics into Features and then Features into Stories. Sometimes, you can split Epics directly into Stories, and that is fine as well.

The key is that, as you are splitting a work item into smaller work items, you get to a point where you have Stories.

"What are Stories?"

These are small bodies of work that the team can take, put into a Sprint, and deliver inside 1 Sprint. Therefore, the expectation is that a Story fits within a Sprint.

The work that Product Management needs to do is to refine the Epics into Features, and Features into Stories. This is part of refinement of the backlog and is often a collaboration between members of the Product Management team (Epic Owners, Product Managers, and Product Owners).

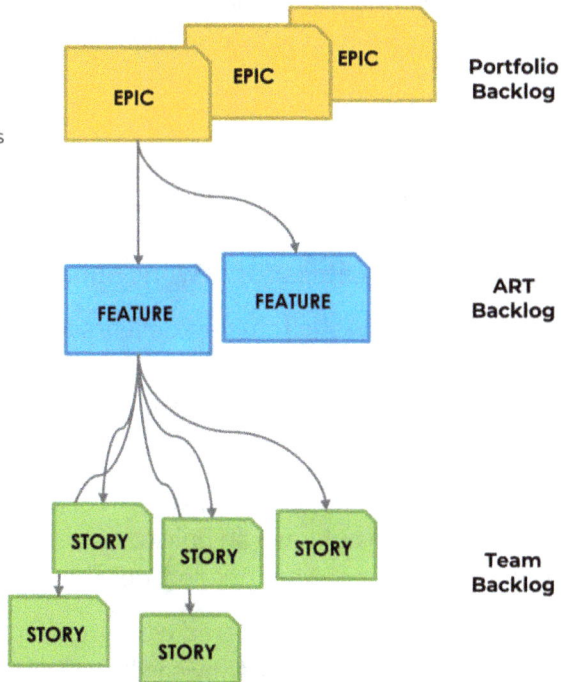

EPIC
Large body of work spanning months (sometimes, multiple quarters). Completed when the Features/Stories are completed.

FEATURE
Large functionalities that typically require multiple Sprints to complete. May be released all at once.

STORY
Small body of work that can be completed within one Sprint and delivers a valuable functionality.

EPIC · EPIC · EPIC — **Portfolio Backlog**

FEATURE · FEATURE — **ART Backlog**

STORY · STORY · STORY · STORY · STORY — **Team Backlog**

Different Backlogs in SAFe

In SAFe, because we have multiple levels and because we have backlogs at different levels, typically the Epics are managed within a Portfolio Backlog. A Portfolio Backlog may contain 10, 20, or 25 different Epics.

Then we go down to the ART (Agile Release Train) level, and we have an ART Backlog, which is a list of prioritized Features.

We can break these into Stories, and then we get to the Team level where each team has its own Team Backlog with a bunch of Stories. Work items in the backlogs are always prioritized so that the teams can execute the work in order of priorities.

What Epics Are Not

Epics are large bodies of work, something that the team needs to do. As such, they have a start date (when the team begins working on the Epic) and an end date (when the work on that Epic is completed and can be released). We may not know the end date when we start working on an Epic (and that is OK), but we understand that, at some point in the future, the work on an Epic will be completed and the Epic itself will be closed.

Epics are Not Categories

A category specifies a description or a group of work items. For example, "new functionalities", "bugs and enhancements", or "technical debt." These are all categories of work. But these are not Epics.

An Epic would be a work item that delivers a new functionality for the end user (e.g., "Allow users to submit a question to the AI (Artificial Intelligence) engine and to get a response"), and this Epic may fall under the "new functionalities" category.

What I often see is that teams try to fit every Story or Feature into an Epic. And if they do not have an Epic to map to, they create one stating a category. But that is neither needed, nor the right way to use Epics.

Epics should always be considered work items in the backlog. And as such, they can be prioritized, they can be refined and broken down into smaller work items, they can be completed and removed from the backlog, and they can be deleted because they are no longer needed.

Instead, a category stays there forever.

If you need to mark work items and to assign them to categories, do not use Epics. Instead use other tools, like tags, or color-coding. This is a more preferable way to manage work.

Epics in Jira

If you are using Jira, in its out-of-the-box configuration it comes with an Epic backlog. You can list here major items you want to implement in your product. And you can map Stories/Tasks to the Epics.

Notice that Jira also shows a completion score on each Epic: how much of that Epic has been completed so far. That is because Jira knows that

Epics are work items (major ones) and tracks their completion rate over time. At some point, an Epic will be done 100% and can be removed from the backlog.

Managing a Portfolio of Epics

The Portfolio Kanban

Because Epics are major items, every time we start working on an Epic, we face the decision:

"Do we want to build the whole Epic? Or do we want to build a small portion of it and see if we can actually deliver the outcome?"

If we deliver the outcome, then we can keep building everything else in that Epic.

One method that SAFe offers to manage a list of possible Epics and to make decisions on which to focus on, is the Portfolio Kanban. It exists at the Portfolio level, and in its essence, it is a Kanban board. The Portfolio Kanban is divided in columns; each column represents a step in the workflow of taking an Epic from idea to completed execution. By using the Portfolio Kanban, Epic Owners are able to create transparency on the status of each Epic, and make more informed decisions on priorities and on capacity allocation.

As Epics go through the Portfolio Kanban, they progress from one column to another:

Funnel: Typically, the first step is the funnel. This is a "catch-all" for new Epics that are open for consideration. These Epics may represent ideas for a new functionality to build into the product, extensions and enhancements, technical debt resolution (Enabler Epics), capabilities that open new business opportunities, or Epics that solve problems with existing solutions. The items in this column are unrefined and not prioritized.

Review: In the review column, you start to refine the Epics. You could use one of the Epic templates discussed before, to distill the details about the specific work or capability represented by the Epic, to define the hypothesis statement, and to establish an initial priority. You can also get an initial estimate, maybe a rough estimate, just to get a sense of how large the Epic may possibly be.

Analysis: When an Epic moves to the analysis phase, you start to develop a deeper understanding about the actual work, its priority, and its estimate. You may start thinking about the possible solutions that you could implement to deliver that Epic. You may choose to define an MVP (a Minimum Viable Product), to run an experiment and to validate a hypothesis about the Epic. This stage should have a WIP Limit (Work in Progress) based on the Epic Owner's capacity, to avoid doing analysis on too many Epics at the same time. And it is a good practice to limit the number of Epics in progress at any given time.

Be mindful that not all approved Epics must be started.

> *"Project thinking (and funding) tends to lead to pushing of work because of the false expectation that once a project is approved, it must be started. This leads organizations to not consider WIP vs capacity, and can easily lead to overloaded staff who are required to do excessive context switching as they move between the multiple projects that they are concurrently assigned to."*

Iain McKenna

Funnel	Review	Analyze	Portfolio Backlog	Implement		Done

Funnel

Container for all ideas for product growth:

- New functionality to build into the product
- Extensions and enhancements
- Capabilities that open new business opportunities
- Epics that solve problems with existing solutions
- Horizon 2 and 3 opportunities under investigation
- Large Enablers/ technical debt resolution items

Review

Refine the understanding of the Epic:

- Create the Epic hypothesis statement
- Preliminary cost estimates and WSJF priority
- Only refine the top portion of the list based on WSJF

Analyze

Prepare to make a go / no-go decision:

- Ideate possible solution alternatives
- Refine cost estimates and WSJF priority
- Define possible MVP
- Create lean business case
- Go/no-go decision

WIP Limit based on the Epic Owner's capacity

Portfolio Backlog

Prioritize limited number of Epics approved for implementation:

- Epics approved and awaiting capacity for execution
- Epics described with hypothesis statement and lean business case
- Prioritized using WSJF
- Limited in number to keep focus on priorities
- Low priority Epics return to Review phase

Implement

Build and evaluate MVP:

- Pivot or persevere decision based on customer results
- Pivot decision sends Epic back to Review/ Analyze for evaluation of next steps

WIP Limit based on ART capacity

Continue Epic implementation:

- Epics with validated hypotheses move to Continue
- Measure value delivered
- Evaluate when enough is built

WIP Limit based on ART capacity

Done

Work on the Epic is completed:

- Moved to Done when work on the Epic is completed
- Done when enough Features are built to deliver the outcome of the Epic
- Done when MVP does not validate hypothesis and Epic is discarded

Portfolio Backlog: The Portfolio Backlog contains a list of Epics that are prioritized for implementation, with the most important one at the top. Typically, because the Portfolio Backlog is limited in size, it is good to use WSJF (Weighted Shortest Job First), to prioritize the Epics. Since WSJF is a time-consuming technique, I believe it is only feasible when you have a limited number of work items (typically, less than 15 or 20).

Implementation: Epics in this column are in the execution phase. This phase is where the Epic is broken down into smaller work items (through refinement), and the smaller work items are then pulled by the ART and by the Agile Teams for implementation. Typically, you start building an MVP first, validate if the solution works, and then decide to continue with the implementation (or maybe not). The MVP tries to answer the question:

"What is it that we can build in a quick and easy way that we can put out there for our customers to use, and to get feedback from the customers to see if this idea works for them, or not?"

Because Epics are large bodies of work, it is often very useful to identify a core MVP to run an experiment and to test whether the Epic makes sense or not, before you commit to building the whole thing. If the idea does not work, you should stop building it and move on to something different.

Done: And when all of the work on that Epic is done, the Epic itself can be considered completed, and we can close it. This may be because the work on the Epic is completed; because you have built enough Features to deliver the outcome of the Epic and you do not need to continue; or because the MVP does not validate the hypothesis and the Epic can be discarded. In any case, you move the Epic to "Done" so that you open up bandwidth to work on other Epics.

By using a Portfolio Kanban like the one presented here, you can create transparency and track where each Epic is, at what stage, and visualize what the teams are working on. The Portfolio Kanban also provides transparency on priorities, visualizing which Epics you are working on, and which are waiting for a future decision.

Use an MVP to Validate the Epic

Let us look a little deeper at the concept of a Minimum Viable Product and how it can be used to run experiments on a possible idea for a solution.

As stated above, the MVP tries to answer the question:

"What is it that we can build in a quick and easy way that we can put out there for our customers to use, and to get feedback from the customers to see if this idea works for them, or not?"

The MVP should be a working product, something that you can put in the hands of customers, and that they can use. However, you do not need to make the MVP available to all customers at once. You can release the MVP to just 10 of your customers, ask them to use it for a period of time, and then give you feedback.

MVPs foster innovation with rapid cycles of validation

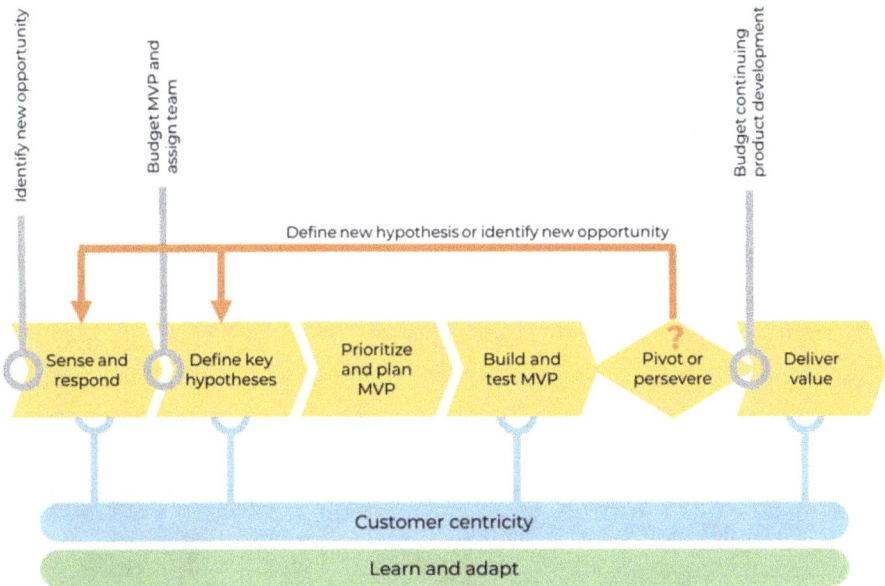

Identify new opportunity

Budget MVP and assign team

Budget continuing product development

Define new hypothesis or identify new opportunity

| Sense and respond | Define key hypotheses | Prioritize and plan MVP | Build and test MVP | Pivot or persevere | Deliver value |

Customer centricity

Learn and adapt

In fact, you do not need a fully working product with a lot of features. The idea behind the MVP is to build just the minimum set of functionalities that allows you to test your product idea for viability.

"What is viability?"

Viability can be defined in customer's and business' point of views:

From the customer's point of view, viability tries to answer these questions:

"Is this product viable for our customers? Is it delivering benefits? Is it solving the customer's problems?"

And there is viability from a business point of view. In this case it tries to answer these questions:

"Can we actually build it? Can we make money out of it? Is this product going to deliver the business outcomes that we expect?"

You build an MVP of your idea, test it with a few customers, and then evaluate it. If the idea does not work, you should stop building it and change the idea. And because Epics are large bodies of work, it is often very useful to start with an MVP of the Epic to test whether the Epic makes sense or not before you commit to building the whole thing.

When you build a new solution to a customer's problem, there are some hypotheses that you are making about the solution itself. You can build an MVP to test these hypotheses. And as a result of that test, you may have two answers:

- **Failure:** the hypothesis is not proven. This MVP does not work, the solution does not work, it is not viable for the customers, and so on. Let us stop working on this; let us pivot instead; let us figure out a different idea; let us do something else. Of course, the sooner you find this out, the better. That is why the Minimum Viable Product needs to be minimum, so you can do that test as soon as possible.

- **Success:** the hypothesis works, and the experiment is successful. Then you can say, let us continue with this idea; let us persevere. You keep building the Epic or the solution; maybe you also have some additional ideas that you want to implement. You keep working with the teams at implementing the solution.

Any Tips on Managing an MVP for an Epic?

By John Mulligan, SPC

What is the smallest thing that you can build to test your Epic hypothesis? Do that.

The advantage Agile methodologies have over waterfall is the ability to iterate, so it is not necessary to think of everything up front. Just do enough to make sure it is feasible, and then build from there.

Support MVPs and Build Epics Incrementally

To see how this works in practice, refer to the picture.

Build Epics incrementally, one PI at a time

Develop first part of the Epic or an MVP

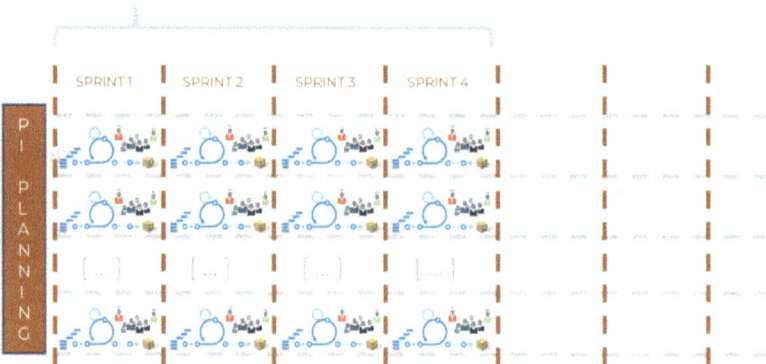

These teams have decided to focus their PI (Planning Interval) on developing the first part of an Epic. Maybe they want to run an experiment or to validate a series of hypotheses, and they decide to build an MVP of that Epic. Either way, at the end of the PI they will have a Product Increment that they have created.

The teams can test it with their customers and with their stakeholders, get feedback, and then decide:

> *"Should we continue building this? Or should we instead build something else?"*

And then they decide in the next PI to develop another part of the Epic (maybe because the experiment was successful) or instead to pivot and to build something else (maybe because the experiment was not successful or priorities have changed).

Build Epics incrementally, one PI at a time

And so, the teams continue their work and build the Epic incrementally along the way.

Example: Shall We Build This Epic?

In this example, we are Product Managers at Netflix (this is a completely fictional example, as I do not work for Netflix, but hopefully this example makes my point).

After some consideration and strategic discussion, the Netflix senior leadership has decided to prioritize a new capability that would allow us to share recommendations for movies with friends. This is defined as an Epic at the Portfolio level:

Epic: Allow subscribers to connect with friends and to share movie recommendations.

This Epic describes a major new functionality to add to the Netflix system. The Netflix senior leadership is convinced that this will make Netflix more interactive, will increase customer engagement with the platform, and will set Netflix apart from its competitors.

They have asked you to prioritize and to build this Epic. What do you do next?

One thing you could do is break down this Epic into some smaller pieces to enable the new functionality.

For example, here are a few Features:

Establish a community of friends on Netflix (create a group of friends; invite friends to join).

Manage the community of friends (add more; remove friends).

Share recommendations for movies with friends in my community.

Receive recommendations for movies from my friends.

Select a recommendation and add it to my watchlist.

Decline a recommendation received from a friend.

The reality, at this moment, is that you do not know if this Epic is really valuable and if you should build it. There are several questions that come to mind, to which we do not have an answer yet:

Would customers find this valuable?

Is the effort required to build this Epic justified in terms of value that we deliver?

Should we build this functionality?

If we build this, will customers use it?

This is the kind of thinking that Product Managers should adopt. Yes, the idea may sound cool. Yes, the idea may come straight down from the executive suite. But it is your job, as Product Manager, to maximize the return over the investment for this idea.

Instead of jumping headfirst into building a large Epic, first spend some time to validate it and to answer these questions. An MVP is a tool to help you do this as quickly and cheaply as possible.

Define the Key Hypothesis

Behind every product idea there is one (or more) hypothesis that you are making about the solution. For example, you may have a hypothesis about the ability of the solution to solve the customer's needs, the feasibility of the solution, the value of the solution for either the business or the customer, or that customers even care enough about the problem to buy your solution.

A key hypothesis is one that – if proved wrong – makes the whole product idea worthless.

For example, let us look again at the Netflix Epic we discussed earlier:

Epic: Allow subscribers to connect with friends and to share movie recommendations.

We may not realize it, but there are some key hypotheses behind this Epic. For example:

- *Hypothesis 1: People care about receiving recommendations from friends.*

- *Hypothesis 2: When people receive recommendations for movies from friends, they actually consider them and watch the recommended movies.*

- *Hypothesis 3: People like to share recommendations and then watch the movie together as a shared experience.*

- *Hypothesis 4: If we build the ability to share recommendations, we will see an increase in engagement on the platform.*

For each hypothesis you define, you should also think about a way in which to evaluate if your solution satisfies or not the hypothesis. And then define one or more metrics you will monitor to decide about the hypothesis.

The flow goes:

Hypothesis   -->   How to evaluate it   -->   Metric to measure

When you build your experiment for hypothesis validation, whether that is an MVP, a prototype, or another form, you now know what to measure and what to look for in order to validate the hypothesis (or not).

The Epic Hypothesis Statement

Because Epics are large bodies of work, we do not want to commit upfront to building the whole thing. Instead, we should find a way to build just a small portion of it, validate that indeed it delivers value to the customers and to the business, and – if it does – decide to build the rest of it. And, if it does not deliver value or does not work for our customers, we should pivot, consider a different solution, or scratch the whole Epic altogether.

Writing Epics from a functional point of view creates the misleading sense of confidence in the actual solution. Instead, writing Epics using a hypothesis statement instills the understanding that we may not know what the best solution is, or may not even know if this Epic makes sense at all. Hence, we need to validate it.

SAFe offers a template that defines these Epics using the Epic Hypothesis Statement[xxiii]. This is a format that you can use to express the desired outcome of an Epic. The Epic Hypothesis Statement helps to answers questions like,

"Why should we build this Epic?"

"What is the value that we are going to deliver?"

The hypothesis in this statement helps to make it clear that if we build this Epic, we are going to deliver this outcome. And because it is a hypothesis, the outcome is not certain and is something that you need to validate.

The Epic Development Form

I often use a slightly different template[xxiv]. This template allows to define some additional details on the Epic that I find useful.

For example, we can try to provide an answer to these questions:

"Who are the users who are going to benefit from this work?

What is the problem that we are going to solve for our customers?

How do we know when the value has been delivered?

This template helps to ground the Epic with a deeper understanding of the customers, their problems, and the success criteria for completion.

Notice that the functional details of the solution are not defined in this template. This also supports the thinking that Epics should be validated before committing to a full build.

Understand the Flow of Value to the Customer

Because an Epic is a large body of work, it likely includes multiple activities that the customers conduct in order to receive value from the solution. Not all of these activities have the same value or importance, and not all are critical to validate a solution. Understanding which steps are more important is key to break down an Epic and to define an MVP.

Understanding the flow of value starts from understanding who the customer is. And then, understand the different steps the customer is taking as they interact with your solution.

What activities are they doing?

What do they need the solution to do?

What needs or pain points are they trying to address?

Operational Value Streams

An Operational Value Stream maps the sequence of activities needed to deliver a solution to the customer.

For example, an Operational Value Stream for Uber may look something like this: Uber first needs to get the customer's location and the destination, then needs to find a driver available, then needs to provide guidance to the driver to pick up the customer and to take the customer to their destination, and finally, it needs to collect payment from the customer and to pay the driver for his service. The Uber system is designed to properly support each of these activities and to make sure that customers can use the solution effectively.

The first step in defining a solution for a customer is to understand the steps in the value stream. By mapping out all of the steps, the product team can understand the different systems involved in providing the solution, the functionalities that need to be built, and the sequence of activities needed to deliver value to the customer.

It is beyond the scope of this book to describe how to define an Operational Value Stream, but many resources are available, including guidance from Scaled Agile on their website[xxv].

Customer Value Stream

A customer value stream is the entire journey your customer takes to receive value and to benefit from your product or service. It essentially maps out of all the steps involved, from the moment they become aware of your offering, to the point when they realize its full value. Notice that this may be broader than the Operational Value Stream: The Operational Value Stream is defined with an internal point of view (the steps we need to support to deliver value), whereas the Customer Value Stream is defined from the customer's point of view. In addition to the operational steps, it may include steps in the acquisition, activation, support, or maintenance phases.

Customer Value Streams or Operational Value Streams?

Both Customer Value Streams (CVS) and Operational Value Streams (OVS) are related concepts that deal with delivering value, but they differ in perspective and in scope:

Perspective:

- **CVS:** Focuses on the **customer journey** and the steps they take to receive value from your product or service. It includes all interactions, touchpoints, and experiences the customer has, even if they involve internal operations.

- **OVS:** Focuses on the **internal operations** necessary to deliver that value to the customer. It maps out the specific activities, departments, and resources involved in turning an order into a delivered product or service.

Scope:

- **CVS:** Broader in scope, encompassing the entire journey from marketing and awareness to purchase, usage, and post-sale support.

- **OVS:** Narrower in scope, focusing on the specific steps within your organization that directly contribute to fulfilling the customer's order.

As Product Managers, we should always adopt an outside-in thinking and develop customer-centric points of view. Understanding and mapping the Customer Value Stream supports this approach.

Customer Journey Map

An effective way to visualize the Customer Value Stream is to create a **Customer Journey Map**[xxvi]. This map starts from identifying a User Persona and then maps out all of the steps in that Persona's journey with your intended solution.

Customer Journey Maps[xxvii] are a visual representation of customer interactions with your business, product, online experience, retail experience, or any combination. These maps are developed from a customer point of view, designed to highlight how customers interact with your brand, product, services, and people. The more touchpoints you have, the more complicated — and useful — such a map becomes.

The map includes the key activities and touchpoints, the pain-points and needs at each step, and the customer's emotional status while they go through the steps. The Customer Journey Map is a wonderful tool that will expand your understanding and will identify areas of value for your customers beyond the strict functional elements of your solution.

A Journey Map may focus on a specific interaction (e.g., a customer who visits your online store to buy a product, or a customer who calls customer service to solve an issue) or may take a broader view through several interactions (e.g., the decision to buy a new car may require an online search, a couple of visits to the dealer, or a visit to the bank).

How Does a Profit Stream™ Help Deliver Value?

By Jason Tanner, CST and Luke Hohmann, SAFe Fellow

A Profit Stream[xxviii] is a value stream designed to create a sustainable business. Profit Streams:

- Quantify the economic value of the solution they create.

- Are sold through pricing and licensing choices that ensure the revenue generated from these solutions exceeds the costs required to serve across the solution lifecycle.

Profit Stream design ensures the sustainability of software-enabled solutions. Profit Stream design integrates three aspects of sustainability, all of which are interdependent and evolve over time:

Solution sustainability:

Customers receive a continuous flow of value. The timing of this flow of value is determined by customer and market needs and the nature of the solution.

The frequency of value delivery is enabled - or constrained - by technical choices in the design and delivery of the solution, compliance requirements, and other contextual factors.

Economic sustainability:

A customer's assessment of value is greater than the price they have paid, and revenues exceed your costs to create, maintain, and operate the solution - which often vary by customer segment.

Selecting your solution also means that it provides more value than alternative solutions, including the status quo.

Relationship sustainability:

The legal agreements (such as contracts, terms and conditions, and licensing agreements) that govern the interactions between the solution, customers, suppliers, and regulatory agencies, promote mutually beneficial outcomes.

What Is the Profit Stream Canvas?

By Jason Tanner, CST and Luke Hohmann, SAFe Fellow

The Profit Stream Canvas[xxix] is organized to help manage the system of interrelated choices involved in designing Profit Streams such as:

- Identifying the economic value of your solution from the perspective of customers.

- Selecting the appropriate value exchange model for your solution.

- Determining the optimal pricing model for your solution.

- Constructing customer ROI models.

- Ensuring customer license agreements align to all other decisions.

Download the Profit Stream Canvas:

https://profit-streams.com/profit-stream-canvas

Identify MVPs With the Product Journey Map

For many product teams, going from an Epic to a minimum set of Features that helps to validate the Epic's MVP, is not an easy task. Some tend to take on too much work and to create a product release that is less of an MVP and more of a full product. Others take the input from the Epic Owner and build whatever they have been asked to, trusting that the Epic Owner has made the right decision. The product team is not empowered to validate a solution and to iterate on it, and instead it works in a top-down hierarchical approach. In either case, the end result is a higher risk of building too much or building the wrong thing, with a waste of money and time.

The Product Journey Map is a useful tool to define the scope of an MVP and to compare it to the overall scope of the solution. It is also useful for creating alignment on what is in-scope and what is not, among all the members of the product team and the stakeholders.

The Product Journey Map

The **Product Journey Map** is a tool that brings together the focus on a User Persona, the Customer Journey, and the key hypothesis, and defines a plan for an MVP. It can be used by Product Management to take an Epic, to break it down into its main parts, and then to decide which parts need to be built into an MVP to validate the Epic. The tool takes its inspiration from User Story Mapping[xxx] (a technique used to map User Stories and to identify relationships / priorities). In this context, it helps to break down a large Epic into the key components that are needed for building an MVP out of it.

Product Journey Map

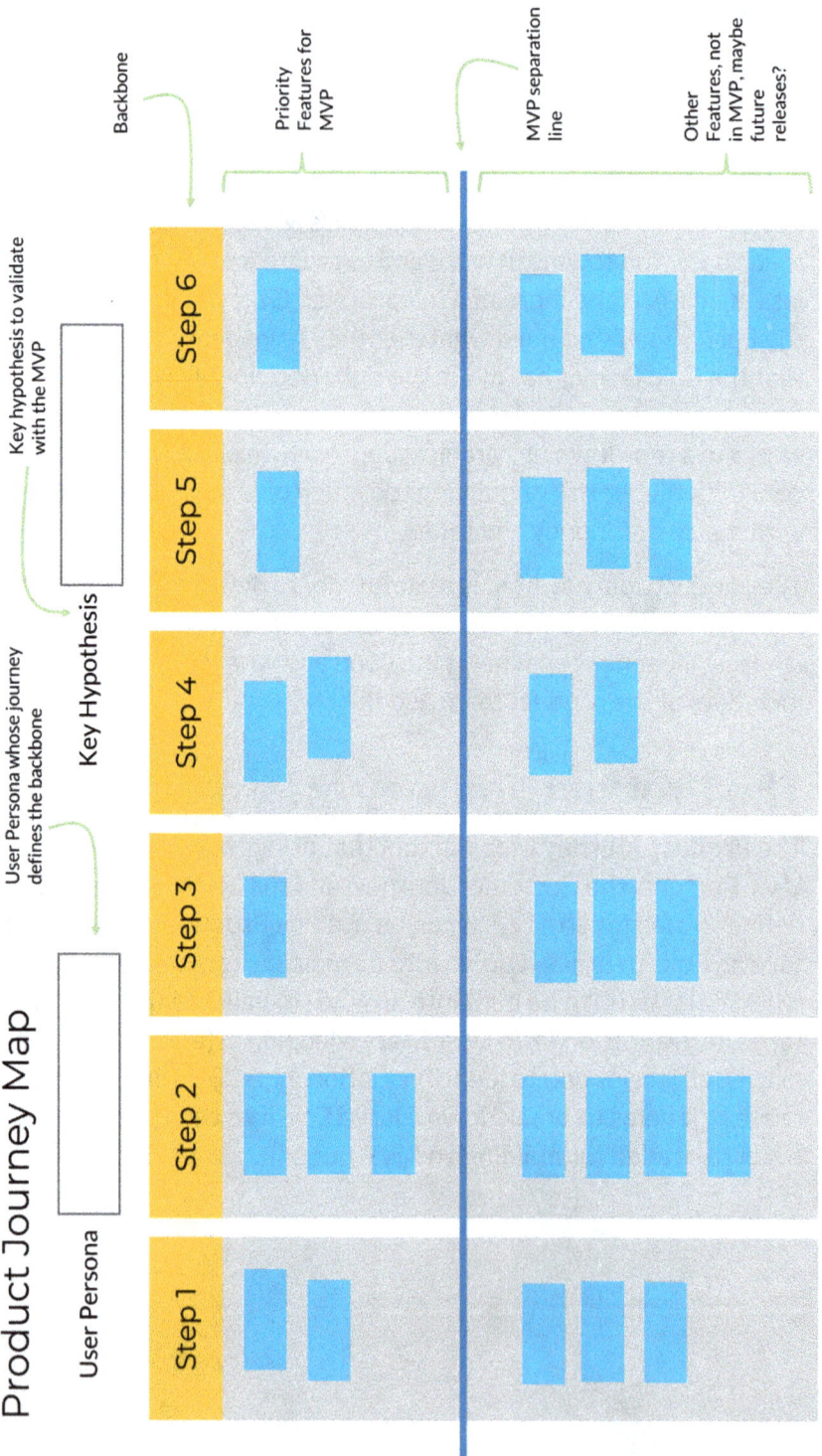

User Persona

Step 1   Step 2   Step 3   Step 4   Step 5   Step 6

Key Hypothesis

User Persona whose journey defines the backbone

Key hypothesis to validate with the MVP

Backbone

Priority Features for MVP

MVP separation line

Other Features, not in MVP, maybe future releases?

How to Build a Product Journey Map

To build a Product Journey Map you can follow these steps:

1 – Start from defining the **User Persona(s)** that you want to focus on. Having a clear idea about your target User Persona gives you a deeper understanding of the inner needs, the aspirations, and the beliefs of your customers and of your target market. And this helps you design a better solution for them.

2 – Identify the steps that define the **backbone of your Product Journey Map.** These define the major areas of functionality or the main needs your customers want to satisfy.

To identify these steps, you can use two approaches:

- **Customer Journey Map:** if you have created a Customer Journey Map, use the steps of this map as a starting point for your backbone. You can always iterate on these, but this is a great way to get started.

- **Value Stream:** if you have an Operational Value Stream (OVS) or a Customer Value Stream (CVS), use the steps in the value stream to define your backbone. While both can work, whenever possible, I prefer to use the CVS as it offers a broader picture of the customer needs and of their interaction with our product or solution.

The steps of your customer's journey become the backbone of the **Product Journey Map.**

3 – It is time to **define what your MVP** will look like. Consider answering these questions:

What is the goal of your MVP?

What are the key hypotheses you need to validate?

What key elements on the technology, business, and human side should you include in your MVP to deliver a full customer experience that validates your hypotheses?

The MVP is a tool to test and validate a solution, therefore the key to a successful MVP lies in the proper identification of the key hypotheses you are making about your solution. You should clearly define what hypotheses you are making about your product idea, and which of these the MVP should help you validate. That is why at the top of the Product Journey Map you see a box for the hypothesis.

If you need to validate a large, or non-overlapping set of hypotheses, you may choose to have more than one MVP. In this case, create multiple variations of the Product Journey Map.

You can also use the **MVP Ideation Canvas**[xxxi] to define your key MVP elements.

4 - Once you have all of the pieces identified, you and your team[xxxii] can brainstorm a **list of Features** you would like to build for each of the steps in your journey. These represent all of the possible Features you may decide to implement in your solution. Go for quantity at this point and defer judgment to a later stage.

5 – Considering the objective of your MVP and the key hypothesis you want to test, you can **prioritize the list of Features.** Move to the top of the list only those that are really necessary to deliver the core experience of your MVP. All others should move down the list to a later stage. You should do this for each column in your map.

6 – **Draw a line** (or use blue tape on the wall if in person) to separate the MVP Features from everything else. Move the core Features you need for the MVP above the blue line. Everything else can be postponed to a future date and moved below the blue line. Having this line visible makes it clear what is in-scope for the MVP and what is not.

The Features above the blue line should be those that you need to validate the hypothesis. If something is not needed, keep it below the blue line. You can always expand your product after you have validated the MVP.

7 – You may draw additional lines to **identify future releases beyond the MVP**. Now your roadmap is taking shape.

However, consider these future plans as "intended plans" and not as "set-in-stone plans". In an Agile world, planning more than 1 or 2 releases ahead may not prove a good use of your time as things may change before you get there.

I have found Product Journey Maps a useful tool to provide visibility to everyone – including the stakeholders and the executives – about the roadmap and what to expect from the MVP. They are also a useful tool to maintain focus on the MVP and to avoid scope creep.

For more information on Product Journey Maps and to download a "how-to guide", visit: https://www.5dvision.com/templates/product-journey-map

Success Story at Capital One

We used the Product Journey Map at Capital One to create alignment and to plan the release of a new strategic enterprise tool. At the start, it was a huge, multi-year endeavor and we did not have senior leadership support (i.e. budget) to cover it all. So, we asked ourselves:

"What is the minimum we can build to deliver an experience that our users would like and to validate a key hypothesis we have on this product?"

We decided to build an MVP, to test it with a few of our bankers, and to see whether our solution delivered the benefits they expected. If that held true, we could go back to senior leadership with a case for an increase in budget and then we could build the full product for everyone.

We created a Product Journey Map on a big wall in the office (we were still in-person at the time), with a horizontal blue line and a list of key features above it for the MVP. We decided to be very strict on those MVP Features given the limited budget we had at our disposal and the need to validate the solution as quickly as possible. We had a core hypothesis that by building a specific new functionality we could change the way in which our bankers interacted with our customers, creating a much richer customer experience.

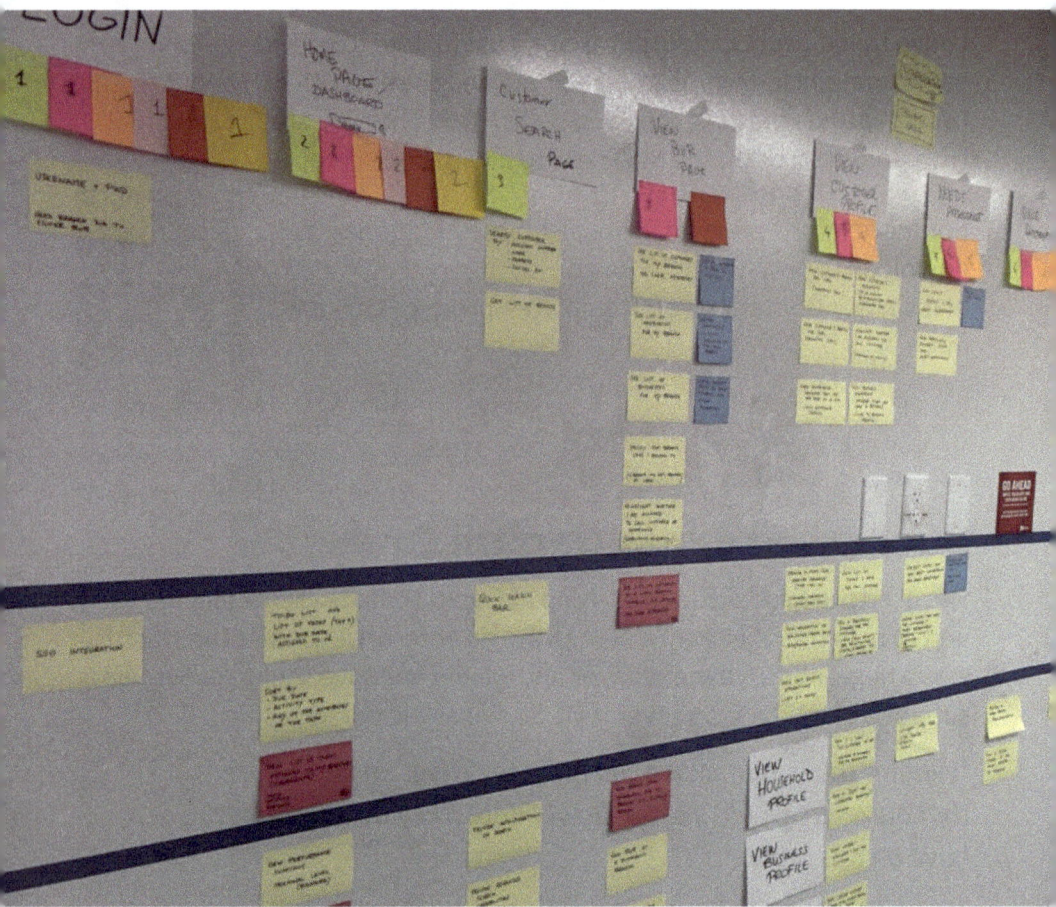
A Product Journey Map color-coded for different User Personas.

In 4.5 months, we were live in production with an MVP. It did just a few things, but these were the things connected to our hypothesis. We validated it and got feedback from both bankers and customers that we were on the right track.

We presented the results of our MVP test to the executives, and we got a larger budget so that we could build the full solution. This set the wheel in motion for building a bigger and more complex tool using a Salesforce platform that could be used by all 5,000 bankers in our bank.

A couple of years later, our product was considered the largest Salesforce implementation in the Financial Services industry to date: It had started with a limited MVP test and had grown from it.

The Product Journey Map allowed this to happen, by creating alignment on the objectives, by defining the priorities, and by keeping the focus on the MVP first, and future releases later.

Managing the ART Backlog

The ART Backlog

In the overall SAFe framework, the ART Backlog (in early releases of SAFe this was called the Program Backlog) plays a pivotal role in orchestrating the rhythm of value delivery for the ART. It serves as the central hub, harboring the work that guides Agile Release Trains toward achieving their shared objectives. The ART Backlog contains the list of Features that are prioritized for work by Product Management. The top priorities are refined by the Agile Teams for delivery in the upcoming PI (Planning Interval).

The ART Backlog is managed by Product Management (more specifically, it is often managed by a Product Manager) who aligns to the vision, decides the list of Features to prioritize, and prepares the overall Roadmap for the ART.

The Features are decomposed into Stories in a collaborative effort between the Product Manager and the Product Owners on the ART. Then, the Stories are moved into each Agile Team's backlog, for planning and for execution by the Agile Teams during the PI.

Managing and refining the ART Backlog requires a skillful hand, balancing strategic vision with tactical execution. A well-refined ART Backlog is essential to the successful implementation of SAFe. Without a clear alignment to the Vision and without a focus on priorities, the work performed by the ART becomes scattered and fragmented, resulting in solutions that are either late to market, or that miss the mark for the customers.

Product Management owns, defines, and prioritizes the ART Backlog

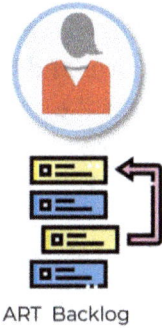

ART Backlog

The Features in the ART Backlog are divided among the teams and decomposed into the Team Backlogs

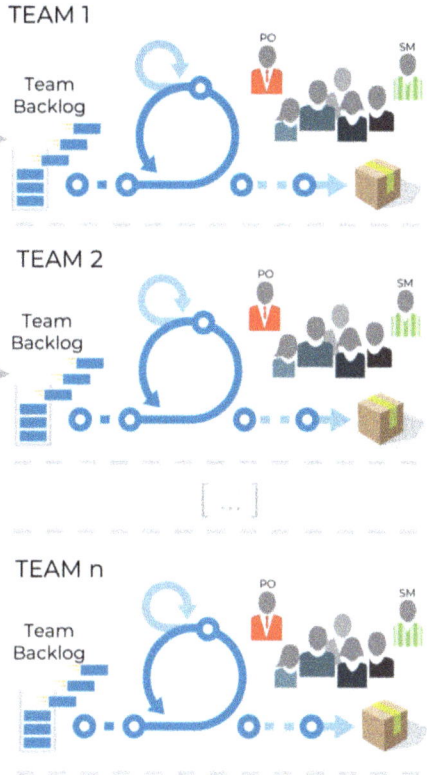

TEAM 1

Team Backlog

TEAM 2

Team Backlog

TEAM n

Team Backlog

That is why the role of Product Management is essential in SAFe as is the adoption of the right product practices: customer discovery and validation, product vision, clear outcomes and metrics, and a focus on priorities. How these practices shape up, depends on the particular organization, and they are all important to drive strategic and tactical decisions on the product. A well-refined and prioritized ART Backlog often results from adopting these practices effectively.

Understanding the ART Backlog

Before diving into the deep end, let us establish our bearings. The ART Backlog exists within a layered structure of backlogs in SAFe. At the top of the hierarchy sits the Portfolio Backlog that contains a list of major initiatives that we call Epics.

Epics get prioritized, refined, and then broken down into smaller parts that describe actionable functionalities and new capabilities that must be built into the system. These work items are called Features and they exist in the ART Backlog. In a sense, the ART Backlog acts as the implementation director, translating the Epics into actionable Features that an ART can bring into development.

The following picture shows the SAFe hierarchy of Epics, Features, Stories, and the corresponding levels for the different backlogs.

EPIC
Large body of work spanning months (sometimes, multiple quarters). Completed when the Features/Stories are completed.

FEATURE
Large functionalities that typically require multiple Sprints to complete. May be released all at once.

STORY
Small body of work that can be completed within one Sprint and delivers a valuable functionality.

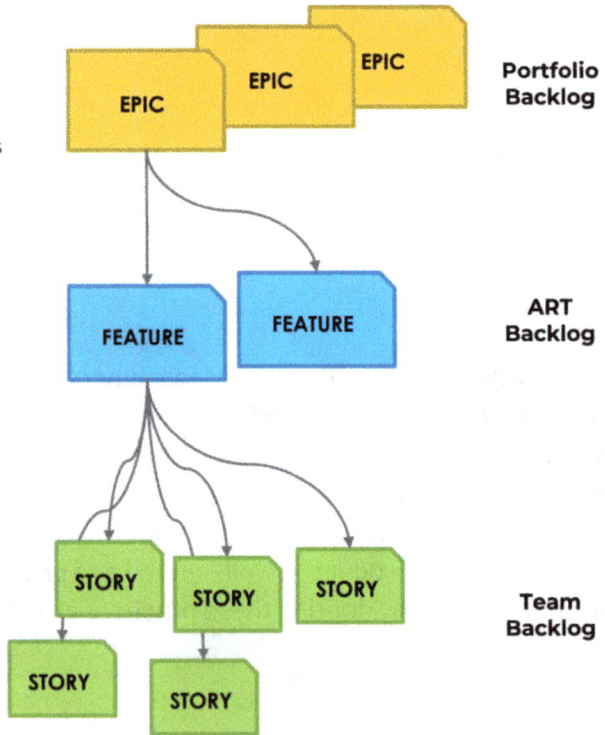

EPIC | EPIC | EPIC — **Portfolio Backlog**

FEATURE | FEATURE — **ART Backlog**

STORY | STORY | STORY | STORY | STORY — **Team Backlog**

Example of ART Backlog

In this example, we pretend to be Product Managers at Netflix (this is a completely fictional example, as I do not work for Netflix, but hopefully this example makes the point).

After some consideration and strategic discussion, the Netflix senior leadership has decided to prioritize a new capability that would allow us to share recommendations for movies with friends. This is defined as an Epic at the Portfolio level:

> **Epic:** Allow subscribers to connect with friends and to share movie recommendations.

This Epic can be broken down into some smaller pieces that need to be built into the Netflix system to enable the new functionality. We can break down the Epic into a list of Features and put them into the ART Backlog:

> **ART Backlog** (list of Features)
>
> Establish a community of friends on Netflix (create a group of friends; invite friends to join).
>
> Manage the community of friends (add more; remove friends).
>
> Share recommendations for movies with friends in my community.
>
> Decline a recommendation received from a friend.
>
> Collect points based on "likes" for recommendations that are provided.
>
> Show a leaderboard of the most active friends in the community.

As you can see, the ART Backlog contains a list of all possible Features needed to create the Epic. Each one of these is a distinct functionality that customers can use. A Feature can be prioritized, it can be scheduled for development, and it can be taken by the Product Owners for execution in a PI.

The job of the Product Manager is to create this list (breaking down the Epics into actionable parts) and then to decide its priorities. Not everything has the same importance, and so the Product Manager needs to decide where to start to deliver the most value faster.

Also, not everything in the ART Backlog needs to be built or does not need to be built all at once. In fact, the Product Manager may decide to prioritize a small subset of Features, to get them done, and then to validate them with customers. Then, based on customer feedback and measured outcomes, decide the next set of Features to build. It means that, at any moment, the ART Backlog may contain some Features that are just "ideas," and the Product Manager will decide whether to build them in the future, or to discard them based on the feedback received by customers.

One example of this is building a minimum viable product (MVP) for a larger Epic. The product manager can select a limited number of features for the MVP, prioritize them for development, and then decide what to build next based on the results.

(You can use Product Journey Maps to define the MVP for the Epic.)

Prioritizing the ART Backlog

Of course, the ART Backlog may contain a long list of Features. Because not all of the Features may be equally important, or because the ART may not be able to work on all of them at the same time, a key activity of Product Management is to prioritize the ART Backlog.

Prioritization is part of the refinement activities that a Product Manager needs to do in order to prepare an ART Backlog for development. In fact, at the start of a new PI, a key input to PI Planning is a prioritized ART Backlog. Without it, the Agile Teams would not know what to work on or where to focus their effort.

The heart of backlog refinement lies in its prioritization. The prioritization of the ART Backlog can be done at any time. In general, it is useful to do it as follows:

Backlog Refinement: Throughout the PI, the ART Backlog is continuously refined. Product Management refines the ART Backlog continuously as it learns of new requests from customers, performs discovery and validation activities, and aligns to the Vision and to other strategic objectives. Epics are decomposed into Features, dependencies are identified, and priorities are reassessed based on emerging insights and on changing business needs. Once a week, Product Management also meets with Product Owners at the ART Sync. This creates alignment and transparency on upcoming priorities and prepares the ART Backlog for the next PI Planning event.

Prepare for PI Planning: In preparation for PI Planning, Product Management defines and prioritizes the list of Features for the upcoming PI. The prioritized list of Features is an input to PI Planning and it is typically finalized in the days leading to the event. The list of prioritized Features is shared with the ART at the onset of PI Planning and this sets the stage for the Agile Teams to craft their own backlogs.

Break-down Features into Stories: In preparation for PI Planning, the Product Management team (Product Managers and Product Owners) should collaborate and refine the ART Backlog together. This gives Product Owners an early look into the Features that will be prioritized for the upcoming PI, and helps them be better prepared for PI Planning.

Weighted Shortest Job First

While many prioritization techniques exist and can be adopted by Product Management, SAFe recommends using the Weighted Shortest Job First (WSJF) technique to prioritize the ART Backlog. The Weighted Shortest Job First is a prioritization technique that generates a numbered priority for each work item in your backlog. The items with the highest numbers have the highest priorities.

It calculates the value for each of the work items expressed as "Cost of Delay" and weighs it against the effort that it would take to build the item, called "Job Size". It considers both the importance of the work (value to business/user) and the relative effort required to complete it (job size). The goal is to identify the items that can deliver the highest value in the shortest time. By factoring in both value and effort, WSJF ensures that the most impactful work gets done first.

$$\text{WSJF PRIORITY} = \frac{\text{COST OF DELAY}}{\text{JOB SIZE}}$$

$$\text{WSJF PRIORITY} = \frac{\text{VALUE} + \text{TIME CRITICALITY} + \text{RISK REDUCTION / OPPORTUNITY ENABLEMENT}}{\text{JOB SIZE}}$$

The three components of Cost of Delay in the numerator, are evaluated Feature by Feature in numerical values:

Value: It represents both the value delivered to the customers and the value generated to the business (in general, for a healthy business these two should not be in contradiction).

Time Criticality (also called Value Reduction Over Time): It specifies if the Feature has a time criticality because its value decreases over time, or because by waiting too long, it may lose its effectiveness. This is often due to competitive reasons in the market or to technology obsolescence.

Risk Reduction or Opportunity Enablement: It quantifies the level of risk that waiting to build that Feature may expose the business to. For example, an upcoming change in regulation may require you to change a Feature in your product by a specific deadline, and failure to doing so may result in hefty fines. Or, by building a Feature we may create a new opportunity in the market or enable the support for more Features in the future. This component in the WSJF formula allows us to prioritize Enablers together with customer Features: Enablers may de-risk the product by removing technical debt or may create new opportunities by extending the architecture runway.

The denominator in the WSJF formula is the Job Size:

Job Size: In WSJF, a backlog item is called a "job." The Job Size is an estimate of the level of effort it would take to complete the job.

The estimate of each component in the formula can be done using standard sizing techniques, such as the modified Fibonacci series (1, 2, 3, 5, 8, 13, 20, 40, 100). This has the advantage of not only being a familiar sizing technique, but is already set in a numerical format, allowing for a quick use of the formula.

Advantages of WSJF

WSJF offers several advantages:

Promotes efficiency: By considering both value and effort, WSJF avoids wasting time on low-value tasks that take a long time. It encourages breaking down large, complex tasks into smaller, more manageable chunks that can be completed faster.

Balances new Features with Enablers and Technical Debt: A typical problem when prioritizing a product backlog is how to properly evaluate the relative importance of technical work (for example, Enablers, Bugs, or Technical Debt) compared to new customer-facing functionalities. WSJF simplifies the approach by evaluating not only the value, but also the time criticality (this could be important for a bug or a new technology) and the risk reduction / opportunity enablement (this could be important for compliance and regulatory work, or technical debt work).

Reduces risk: WSJF balances new functionalities with tasks that mitigate risks or create new opportunities. This proactive approach helps ensure potential problems are addressed early and new opportunities are not missed.

Provides objectivity: WSJF uses a numerical approach based on relative values and effort estimates. This helps remove bias and subjectivity in the prioritization process. Priorities are expressed as numbers and be easily ordered to identify the most important one.

How to Calculate WSJF

To calculate WSJF follow the procedure:

Step 1. Start with "Value." Identify the item in your backlog that has the lowest Value. Assign this item a Value of 1, as this becomes your baseline for the column Value.

Step 2. Estimate all of the items in comparison to the baseline. Once you have completed the "Value" column, repeat the process for the second column, "Time Criticality" and then for the column, "Risk Reduction." Add them up to obtain "Cost of Delay."

Step 3. Finally, repeat the process for the column "Job Size," starting with the item with the smallest effort, and then move on to all of the other items.

Step 4. Calculate WSJF for each item: add up Value + Time Sensitivity + Risk Reduction/Opportunity Enablement, and divide by Job Size. This is the WSJF score for each of the items. The highest score indicates the highest priority.

Example of WSJF Prioritization

Looking back at the Netflix ART Backlog we created earlier, we can use WSJF to identify the priorities in that list. Let us imagine that, after applying WSJF, the results look like the table below.

Feature	Cost of Delay	Job Size	WSJF Priority
Establish a community of friends on Netflix (create a group of friends; invite friends to join).	5	8	0.63
Manage the community of friends (add more; remove friends)	**8**	**5**	**1.60**
Share recommendations for movies with friends in my community.	**13**	**5**	**2.60**
Decline a recommendation that is received from a friend.	1	1	1.00
Collect points based on "likes" for recommendations that are provided.	3	5	0.60
Show a leaderboard of the most active friends in the community.	2	8	0.25

In this example, the two Features in boldface have the highest WSJF scores, and they should be our priorities. Notice that priorities do not account for dependencies. If a Feature requires another one to be implemented, and if the other one has a lower priority score, it may still be done first because of the dependency.

Therefore, the WSJF scores (or the results of any other prioritization technique) should be considered informative, not prescriptive: the Product Manager needs to make the final decision on the order of Features in the ART Backlog, considering all of the data available, including the priorities and any dependencies.

Download a practice exercise for WSJF: https://www.5dvision.com/post/practice-wsjf-prioritization/

When Not to Use WSJF

When the Backlog Is Too Large

WSJF is an effective technique at the Epic or Feature level because typically there are only a limited number of items to prioritize. When the backlog becomes too large, WSJF becomes too complex to use. My personal threshold is around 15 – 20 items. If my backlog is larger than that, I prefer to trim the backlog first, then apply WSJF.

To trim a large backlog, you can use any number of techniques, including Impact-Effort Mapping, or MoSCoW.

Avoid WSJF on the Team Backlog

Another example of when to avoid WSJF is the Team Backlog: typically, a Team Backlog contains a large number of Stories. Again, this makes using WSJF too complex. In addition, at a Team Backlog level, there may be other considerations that play into the ordering of the backlog, including dependencies, and capacity allocation to bug/enhancements or technical debt work.

Therefore, to help Product Owners define priorities for the Team Backlog, I suggest:

Align to the Feature priorities: Product Owners can align with Product Management to ensure that the priorities in the Team Backlog align to the priorities defined for Features.

Consider internal dependencies: Some Stories may need to be completed before others because of dependencies.

Consider inter-team dependencies: Other teams may depend on your work, and you may align your priorities to their needs.

Focus on the goal: Whether you have defined a Product Goal or a set of PI Objectives, you may want to keep the focus on these objectives and prioritize the backlog accordingly.

Tips to Manage the ART Backlog

Mastering the ART Backlog is more an art than a science. By understanding its role, by applying effective prioritization techniques, by utilizing the right tools, and by fostering strong collaboration, you can leverage this backlog to drive your ART toward delivering continuous value.

There are many ways to manage an ART Backlog. The key is to have the list of Features readily available to make decisions on priorities and on any dependencies. In fact, the ART Backlog needs to be visible not only to Product Management (the role responsible for managing it) but also to System Architects, RTEs (Release Train Engineers), and Product Owners, so that everyone has a full picture of what we are trying to build and what is coming up next.

Format of Features

SAFe doesn't prescribe a specific rigid format for Features, but it outlines key characteristics and recommended information to include. Here's a breakdown of what a Feature in SAFe typically entails:

Description: A concise description of the functionality or service the Feature delivers. This should be clear and understandable for everyone.

Benefit Hypothesis: A statement outlining the expected measurable benefit the feature will bring to the end user or the business. This helps focus on the "why" behind the feature and should answer the question:

What value or outcomes will we generate if we build this Feature?

Acceptance Criteria: Specific criteria that define when the feature is considered complete and functional. These criteria should be objective and measurable to ensure successful implementation.

Consider a Set of Experiments

Because Epics represent large bodies of work described by a fundamental hypothesis about a possible solution, and Features are decompositions of Epics, it derives that Features too require validation.

In fact, we should treat Features more like experiments, rather than work orders. We should validate whether a Feature delivers the expected outcome before committing to building the entire functionality. This is highlighted by the Benefit Hypothesis.

If you have followed my reasoning about validating Epics before committing to building them, you see how the same principles apply to validating Features.

The job of Product Management, in collaboration with Product Owners, is to decompose a Feature, to identify the core pieces that need validation, and then to run an experiment to see whether building the whole Feature actually makes sense.

This mindset supports and reflects an agile way of working.

This also makes the job of Product Owners harder than – let us say – traditional Project Managers. In traditional project management, typically, a solution is given from the top and the Project Manager is responsible to deliver that solution within the constraints of budget, scope, and time.

> *"In a product team, you celebrate when you solve a problem."*

> Marty Cagan

Product people understand that solutions are not given. Problems are given (and if they are not clear, we should define them), and then solutions need to be identified. Any problem may have multiple possible solutions. The job of Product Managers and Product Owners, therefore, transforms from *"building a solution that was given by someone else"* to *"finding out the best solution to a given problem"*. This approach requires a different way of thinking, and a different expertise.

174

Collaboration

Remember, managing the ART Backlog is not a solo endeavor. Effective collaboration is paramount. The Product Manager should foster strong relationships with:

Epic Owners: These individuals represent the Epics in the Portfolio Backlog and provide valuable insights to inform prioritization.

Release Train Engineer: The RTE works closely with Product Management to ensure that the ART Backlog aligns with the ART's capabilities and capacity.

System Architects: Leverage their expertise to identify and to address technical dependencies across the backlog.

Product Owners: The Product Owners (POs) drive development with the Agile Teams and they are key partners of Product Management to ensure the delivery of value. The PO Sync is a vital meeting that sets the heartbeat of the Product Management – Product Owners collaboration.

Continuous Improvement

The ART Backlog is a living artifact, evolving with each PI. It is influenced by the priorities set for Epics at the Portfolio level, by strategic objectives, by the Product Vision, by Enablers, by technical dependencies, and by the continuous discovery activities with customers.

Embrace continuous improvement with:

Retrospectives: Regularly reflect on what worked well and what could be improved in managing the backlog.

Experimentation: Be open to trying new techniques and tools to see what optimizes the flow of value.

Leverage MVPs: Break down a major functionality to its key elements and core hypothesis. Then, only build the functionality that allows you to test the hypothesis and validate that the Epic itself is worth building. If customers don't like the idea, pivot as soon as possible and consider a different solution.

Feedback Loops: Actively seek feedback from stakeholders and from customers, and adapt the backlog based on their input. A key event that provides this kind of input is the System Demo. Of course, you do not need to wait for it as you can continually solicit feedback and input from stakeholders and from customers to inform decisions on your backlog.

Additional Suggestions

Here are a few tips to enable proper management of the ART Backlog:

Product Goal: Clearly define a Product Goal (an objective you would like to achieve with your product within the next 3 to 6-ish months) and then make sure that the Features in your backlog align to that Product Goal. The Product Goal can be expressed with PI Objectives.

Kanban Boards: Visualize the work on the backlog using Kanban boards to track progress, to identify bottlenecks, and to ensure transparency. If you are using collaboration tools like Miro or Trello, putting your backlog on a Kanban Board in these tools can make it readily visible to everyone.

Features and Key Outcomes: When defining the Features in your backlog, do not describe just the functionality, but also define the expected outcome(s) that the Feature should deliver to the customer or to the business. SAFe suggests using the Feature Hypothesis Statement to describe the outcome as a hypothesis. This allows you to test if the Feature you have built actually delivers that outcome or not.

Dependencies and Risks: Explicitly map dependencies between Features and proactively manage risks to avoid disruptions. See the Risk Card in a previous chapter.

Metrics and Reporting: Monitor progress towards the PI Objectives and the development of each Feature using the ART Board and the PI Burn-Up Chart.

Use the Epic Backlog in Jira: Out of the box, Jira does not support Features per se. However, it offers Epics and an Epic backlog. For SAFe implementation where having a separate Portfolio Backlog is not necessary (e.g., because you are building just one product), you could list your Features in Jira as Epics and manage your ART Backlog as an Epic Backlog within the tool (it requires a little twist in terminology, but

176

the principles remain the same). When you do this, you can have an at a glance view of the priorities in the Epic Backlog, and you can map the Stories for each Epic to the team's backlog.

Prioritize the Backlog at Least Every PI: At least once per PI (typically, right before PI Planning) prioritize the ART Backlog to identify the key Features that are priorities for the upcoming PI. Then, meet up with the Product Owners in the ART and refine these Features into Stories.

Align to a Roadmap

A product roadmap is a strategic plan that outlines the long-term objectives for a product and details the actionable steps to achieve them over time.

> "A roadmap is a strategic communication tool that clarifies the product vision and development direction."

Teresa Torres

A roadmap provides a view into the future about how we intend to execute on the vision and build the product. Being a plan, the roadmap is never set in stone: it should be considered a living document that is updated at regular intervals to reflect updates in objectives, timeframe, and strategy:

High-level direction: A product roadmap sets the overall direction for the product, similar to how a plan defines the course of action for a project.

Prioritized initiatives: It prioritizes the key Features and functionalities to be developed, just like a plan prioritizes tasks and actions based on importance and urgency.

Phased approach: A roadmap often breaks down development into phases or releases, mirroring how a plan might outline different stages for achieving a goal.

Adaptability: Product roadmaps acknowledge the need to be adaptable. Unexpected challenges or market shifts might necessitate adjustments to the roadmap, just as a plan might need to be revised based on unforeseen circumstances.

The roadmap and the ART Backlog are closely connected with each other: a roadmap should take in consideration the objectives and priorities identified for the product, and the ART Backlog should represent the list of priorities to execute the work defined in the roadmap.

A good roadmap though, is not limited to a list of Features for the product. Instead, it should start by highlighting the key objectives that you want to achieve with the product (these could be expressed as outcomes, or as OKRs). By doing this, you create alignment on the objectives. The Features then become secondary and represent a possible way to achieve those objectives (specific Features may change as we learn more about the solution and what to build to achieve the objectives).

Can You Share a Few Tips to Manage a Roadmap?

By Jason Tanner, CST and Luke Hohmann, SAFe Fellow

A roadmap clarifies and communicates how Product Managers intend to execute on key strategies needed to achieve their goals over a period of time. Roadmaps evolve over time based on the dynamic interplay between the solution and the larger context in which the solution exists. This evolution perfectly captures the balance between creating a plan for the future while responding to reality.

- Build the roadmap collaboratively – with engineers, architects, marketing, sales, customer support – whoever is relevant for the success of your solution. We all need to align on who we're serving, when and how.

- Be clear about what market segment is served over time.

- Explicitly identify the benefits customers will realize from the features of the solution as they are added to the roadmap.

- Consider market *rhythms*, predictable, repeating events of your market, and one time market *events* that are likely to influence your solutions. Then define the *market windows* that drive the highest opportunities for the success of your solution.

- Determine how the technical architecture will evolve to support the delivery of value over time and ensure solution sustainability.

Managing PI Objectives and Risks

PI Objectives

The PI Objectives describe the goals that each team wants to accomplish by the end of the PI. They try to answer the question,

"What goal, or what objective are we trying to achieve in the next 4 to 6 Sprints?"

The PI Objectives can be defined in a few different ways:

They can be expressed as the outcomes that we want to deliver to our customers or to our business with the work that we will do in the PI.

"What problem are we going to solve for our customers?"

"What new opportunity are we creating?"

"What value are we delivering?"

PI Objectives can describe the outcome of a major functionality that we aim to deliver to customers in the PI. Objectives may represent a set of features aggregated together; they could be a milestone that we want to achieve; they could include enabler features, like, for example, completing a major refactoring. For example: *"Deliver the first release of our AI Engine to provide automatic responses to customer support."* That seems to be a pretty good goal to achieve.

Another way to frame the objectives is by using OKRs.

"What is an OKR?"

It is a set of Objectives and Key Results. The idea is that it is not enough to state an objective. We need a key result too.

"How do we know if and when we have achieved it?"

"What do we need to measure to know if we have achieved it?"

The OKRs create transparency and clarity on the objective by adding the key results that we are going to measure if we have delivered that objective or not.

Why Set Objectives?

In her book, *Radical Focus: Achieving Your Most Important Goals with Objectives and Key Results* (2016), Christina Wodtke advocates the use of OKRs in order to achieve focus and to ensure that key goals are realized. The process of identifying and agreeing on objectives and key results is a team effort. Teams can start by clearly articulating and by sharing the business objective. Then, they can set the key results that they believe would help them achieve the company goal.

Wodtke[xxxiii] says,

> *"Goals should not be too easy or too hard.*
> *If goals are too easy, they don't require*
> *enough effort. If they are too hard, people*
> *may avoid any effort at all."*

Setting PI Objectives helps to shift the mind from producing outputs (a feature factory) to delivering outcomes (product thinking). Features (and User Stories) are no longer the goal of the team; rather, they are instruments in achieving an objective.

Each PI focuses on achieving specific objectives.
They are called PI Objectives.

PI Objectives provide guidance during the PI and
establish performance goals for the team

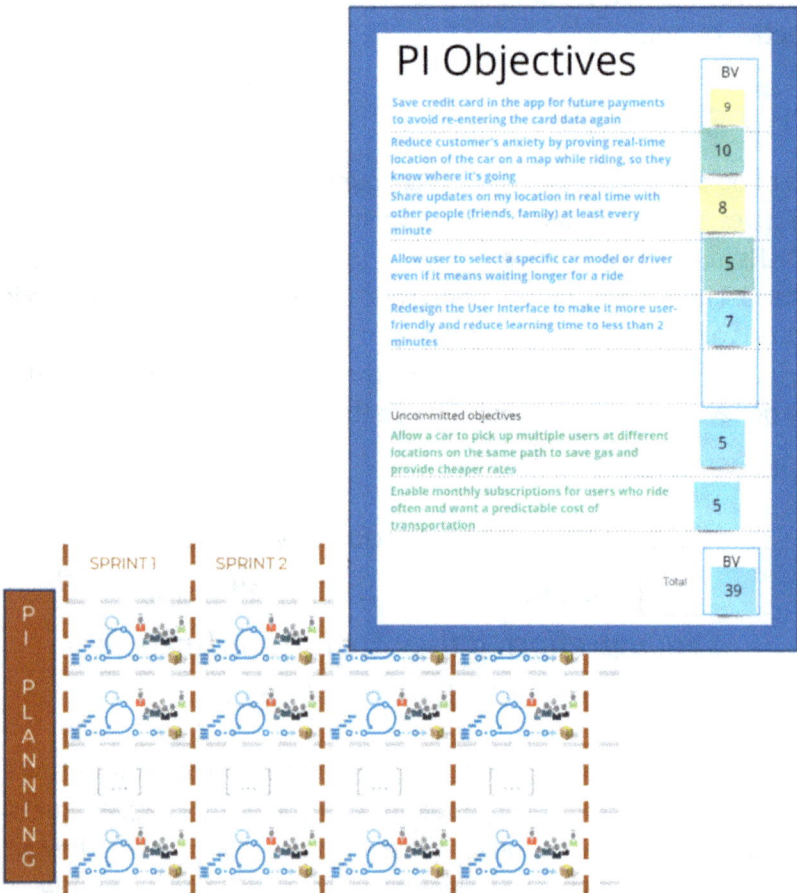

PI Objectives

	BV
Save credit card in the app for future payments to avoid re-entering the card data again	9
Reduce customer's anxiety by proving real-time location of the car on a map while riding, so they know where it's going	10
Share updates on my location in real time with other people (friends, family) at least every minute	8
Allow user to select a specific car model or driver even if it means waiting longer for a ride	5
Redesign the User Interface to make it more user-friendly and reduce learning time to less than 2 minutes	7

Uncommitted objectives

	BV
Allow a car to pick up multiple users at different locations on the same path to save gas and provide cheaper rates	5
Enable monthly subscriptions for users who ride often and want a predictable cost of transportation	5

	BV
Total	39

SPRINT 1   SPRINT 2

P
I

P
L
A
N
N
I
N
G

Different Types of Objectives

Good objectives describe the end state of what you want to achieve. They don't list a series of activities to accomplish, but rather define what the accomplishment will look like. In a sense, they describe the destination, not the route we will take to get there.

Once you are clear about the end state, you can define metrics and baseline values to measure if you are making progress and getting there. In order to define these metrics though, we need to know what the end state should look like, or what is the outcome that we want to achieve.

Objectives can be customer-centric or business-centric:

Customer objectives represent what we want to achieve for our customers, what we want our customers to be able to do with the product, or new behaviors that we want to create with our customers. Notice that the keyword here is "customer": in defining these objectives, we should take the customer's perspective and understand what they want to achieve.

Business objectives are internal outcomes that we want to achieve that are valuable for our business. These may be related to enabling new capabilities, to reducing friction in a process, or to enabling a new revenue stream.

A third category of objectives is represented by team objectives:

Team objectives represent what we want to achieve for our own team, for example, to improve how we work together, or to reduce technical debt to improve the performance of the team. Enablers may support team objectives.

In defining your objectives for a PI, you may identify a combination of different types of objectives.

SMART Objectives

One good practice to frame the objectives is to use the SMART objectives framework.

"What are SMART objectives?"

SMART[xxxiv] stands for Specific, Measurable, Achievable, Relevant, and Time-bound. It is a mnemonic acronym that is used to guide the setting of goals and objectives:

Specific: The objective should be specific and clearly defined.

"What exactly do you want to achieve?"

Measurable: The objective should be measurable so that you can track your progress and determine when you have achieved it.

"What metrics will you use to measure your success?"

For example, the KR (Key Results) part of an OKR can specify how to measure the objective.

Achievable: The objective should be achievable, but challenging. It should be something that you can realistically achieve with the resources and time that you have available. It should not be impossible.

Relevant: The objective should be relevant to your overall goals and strategy. It should be something that is worth achieving and that will help you to achieve your overall goals. For example, the objective may be related to the Product Goal or to the overall Product Vision for the product.

Time-bound: The objective should have a specific deadline.

"When do you want to achieve it?"

Typically, this is by the end of the PI, but you can set an earlier date.

By setting SMART objectives, you can increase your chances of success and achieve your goals more effectively.

Committed Objectives

The PI Objectives that the team establishes during PI Planning are intended as a commitment on behalf of the team (unless otherwise specified). In general, when the team defines the objectives that it would like to achieve for the PI, it establishes a commitment on achieving those objectives.

By defining a PI Objective, the team is inherently communicating that it commits to that objective and that it will do its best to achieve it.

Uncommitted Objectives

In some situations, there could be some objectives that we feel are important and that we want to work on, but that we cannot commit to. We want to do our best, but we feel a little bit uncertain about these objectives, for example, because we do not have all of the information needed or the necessary support. We may call out these objectives as "uncommitted."

When we do this, we are signaling that we do not feel completely certain that we can deliver them 100%. If we have uncommitted objectives, they remain important and part of the plan. They are not a "stretch goal" or "best wishes." No, they are objectives that we intend to achieve in the PI, and we are signaling that we feel less than 100% confidence in our ability to delivering them completely.

Identifying and Tracking Risks

The work that Agile Teams do is very complex. And, given the complexity, there are always risks. It does not help anyone to sweep the risks under the carpet and to hope nobody notices.

Instead, risks should be brought up to the surface, so that we can discuss them and possibly identify solutions to mitigate them.

Risk management is the process of identifying, assessing, and controlling threats to an organization's capital, earnings, and operations[xxxv]. Risks can come from many sources, including financial uncertainties, legal liabilities, technology issues, strategic management errors, accidents, natural disasters, and access to resources.

Here are a few examples:

- We may not be able to complete the work because of [insert xyz reason].

- What we do, may not work out for our customers.

- There could be a cyber security risk with hackers disrupting our network.

- If we have suppliers, the supply chain may not work or we may not get the supplies that we need in order to do the work on time.

- We have a dependency on [xyz team] and that team may not be able to complete its work for us on time.

- The U.S. market may hit a recession and that will affect our business because of [xyz reason].

The first known cases of risk management date back to ancient times[xxxvi]. Some historians believe that the concept of risk management originated from merchant insurance or gaming.

The Importance of Managing Risks

Managing risks in a project is crucial for its success for several reasons[xxxvii]:

Increased Predictability and Control: By proactively identifying and analyzing potential roadblocks, you can anticipate challenges and make informed decisions to avoid or mitigate their impact. This leads to smoother project execution and lessens surprises.

Improved Project Outcomes: Risks like budget overruns, missed deadlines, or technical issues can derail your project. Effectively managing these risks increases the likelihood of achieving your project goals on time, within budget, and to the desired quality.

Enhanced Stakeholder Confidence: Openly addressing and managing risks demonstrates accountability and professionalism to stakeholders like clients, investors, or sponsors. This builds trust and confidence in your ability to handle unexpected situations.

Cost Savings: Proactive risk mitigation is often cheaper than tackling problems after they occur. Identifying and addressing potential issues early can prevent costly delays, rework, or redeployment of resources.

Increased Adaptability and Agility: A dynamic risk management plan allows you to adapt to changing circumstances and react quickly to unforeseen events. This agility helps you navigate complex projects and seize unexpected opportunities.

These are some of the reasons we want to identify risks during PI Planning, and then we want to manage them. Let's see a few techniques we can use to identify risks:

Use a Pre-Mortem

A pre-mortem (or premortem) is a meeting or an exercise done at the beginning of a project to proactively identify potential risks and pitfalls that could lead to failure. In essence, it is imagining that the project has already failed and then working backward to understand what caused it.

The key to a successful pre-mortem is in the priming question:

"Imagine that the project has failed. What led to its failure?"

This approach helps teams:

- Identify potential risks they might otherwise overlook: By shifting their perspective to one of failure, participants can uncover issues they might not have considered when focusing on success.

- Discuss risks openly and honestly: The hypothetical nature of the pre-mortem encourages free and open discussion about potential problems without fear of blame or negativity. It also increases psychological safety by creating a space for everyone to think and to share negative thoughts that otherwise would not have been shared.

- Develop contingency plans: By anticipating potential problems, teams can create plans to mitigate or to avoid them, increasing the chances of success.

- Increase confidence: Everyone feels more confidence in the plan.

- Shared vocabulary: It creates a shared vocabulary to talk about things that could go wrong.

Find Your Tigers

Tigers are magnificent animals. And they represent terrible dangers for anyone venturing into the jungle.

In risk management, a "tiger" is a significant risk that may derail or harm an initiative or a project. Therefore, identifying the tigers is a critical step in the management of risks.

However, not all tigers are real risks. So, the "Tiger, Paper Tiger, and Elephant"[xxxviii] approach can help identify and rank the risks. In risk management, these terms are used to categorize potential threats based on their perceived severity and difficulty to overcome:

- **Tiger:** A significant and imminent threat that, if not addressed, will likely cause major harm. It requires immediate attention and substantial resources to mitigate.

- **Paper Tiger:** A threat that appears significant but is ultimately unsubstantiated or easily overcome. This may be something that someone else may worry about, but it does not worry you. It may require some investigation but should not cause major concern.

- **Elephant:** This is the so-called elephant in the room that no one is talking about. It may be a large and complex threat that is difficult to address directly. It requires careful planning, long-term solutions, and may involve breaking down the issue into smaller, more manageable pieces.

The Risk Card

Risks should be evaluated on their impact (e.g., are they Tigers, Paper Tigers, or Elephants?) and on the likelihood of them happening (can we expect this to happen very likely or is it a rare occurrence?).

To help with the identification of risks and the analysis of their impact and likelihood, teams can use the Risk Card template[xxxix].

Download the Risk Card:
https://www.5dvision.com/templates/risk-card

RISK CARD

HOW TO USE THIS CANVAS
Capture the essential risks of your product or project.
Use one card per risk.

DESCRIPTION OF THE RISK

Describe the risk, challenge, or threat as you see it

TIGER
A substantial threat that may kill us

PAPER TIGER
Appears significant, but it does not worry you

ELEPHANT
Large or complex threat, difficult to assess directly

LIKELIHOOD OF IT HAPPENING

LOW — HIGH

IMPACT IF IT HAPPENS

LOW — HIGH

POSSIBLE PATH TO RESOLUTION OR CONTROL

OWNER OF THE CONTROL / RESOLUTION

STATUS

RESOLVED

OWNED

ACCEPTED

MITIGATED

190

Typically, risks are written on red stickies and added to a risk board during PI Planning. The Risk Card provides a deeper understanding and some additional information, compared to a plain red sticky.

For example, it provides a description of the risk, an estimate of the likelihood of the risk to happen, and an estimate of the impact if the risk happens. And it also allows you to start thinking about what possible path can resolve the risk or to control its impact.

ROAMing the Risks

Once we identify a risk, we can start discussing strategies and an action plan to control the risk. For example, we could use the ROAM[xl] approach:

Resolve: We can find a path to resolution and the risk becomes resolved.

Own: We can identify an owner of the risk, somebody who is better suited or volunteers to take ownership of the risk and to do some activities to minimize its impact.

Accept: Maybe we realize that the risk is real, but it is out of our control, so we just decide to accept it (e.g., the impact of a recession on our business).

Mitigate: Maybe we know that the risk cannot be completely avoided, but that there is something we can do to mitigate its impact (e.g., we cannot stop all possible hacking attempts, but we can install firewalls and intrusion detection systems to minimize the probability of an attack).

In conclusion, managing risks in a project is not about eliminating all uncertainty, but rather about actively preparing for potential challenges and developing strategies to minimize their impact. By adopting risk management, you can significantly increase your project's chances of success and build a more resilient and adaptable team.

Tracking Work

Velocity Is Not a Measure of Performance

Agile teams often track the amount of work that they complete during each Sprint with a Velocity measure. This is a useful measure for planning a Sprint, but Velocity does not tell much about the overall progress. For example:

"How are we doing on the PI Objectives we have committed to deliver?"

"Will we be able to deliver everything we had planned by the end of the PI, or are we too late?"

Velocity alone cannot answer these questions.

In fact, Velocity is a planning measure. Because it measures the amount of work completed in prior Sprints, teams can take the average of the last 3 to 5 Sprints, and use this as a baseline for the available capacity in the next Sprint (accounting for team members' availability, a capacity buffer, and any other factors that may decrease capacity for the Sprint). This is a good practice for planning a Sprint and for defining the amount of work for the Sprint Backlog.

But what Product Owners need is a way to track progress over multiple Sprints, and to evaluate if the team is on track to deliver on the objectives (or not).

Tracking Progress with a PI Burn-up Chart

When you have a large body of work that you need to deliver over multiple Sprints (whether that being a new Release, or the work planned for an entire PI), the PI Burn-up Chart is a useful tool to track the progress Sprint by Sprint, until the end of the PI.

PI Burn-up Chart

Depicts the amount of work completed in a PI, Sprint by Sprint.

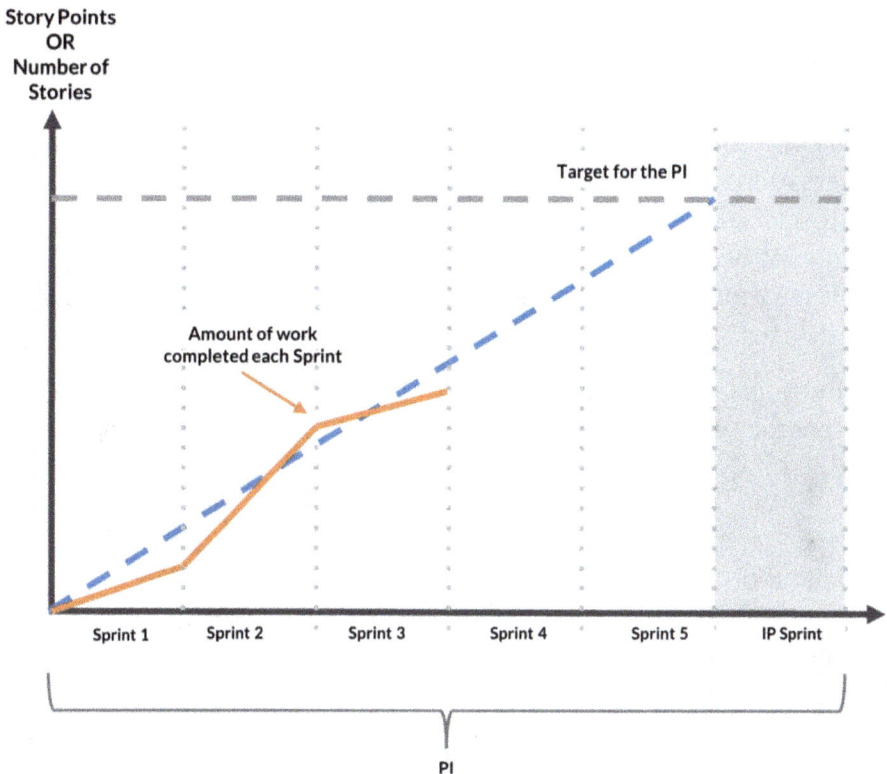

As the team completes a Sprint, it shows on the Burn-up Chart how much work it has completed that Sprint. This is cumulative (it adds to the work completed in prior Sprints). This can be represented in the number of Story Points completed, or in the number of PBIs (Product

193

Backlog Items) completed. Either way is fine, as long as you keep it consistent.

The work completed is compared to the "target" which represents the total amount of work planned by the team for the PI. In theory, the target is established at PI Planning and remain constant. In reality, it changes over the duration of the PI as new requests come in, work is updated, and Stories may be changed. The horizontal line representing the target changes (up or down) to reflect any changes in scope for the PI.

As you track your progress on the Burn-up Chart, you may notice that there is a dotted diagonal line in the chart. This is the ideal trend line, and it represents the trend if you were completing work in a linear way. In reality, this (almost) never happens, as the team's Velocity varies from Sprint to Sprint. However, the ideal trend line gives you a reference for how your Burn-up Chart should (ideally) look.

If you notice that you are deviating from it, you may consider having a conversation with the team, and maybe your stakeholders, to decide how to address the work or to possibly change the plan. In fact, if you are running behind (your chart is below the ideal trend line) you may consider a reduction of the scope of work and a discussion on the key priorities to focus on.

The Burn-up Chart is a useful tool to track the progress and to create transparency with the stakeholders on the team's progress during the PI.

A similar tool can be used by Product Management to track the progress of Features during the PI. The target is represented by the total number of Features planned for the PI. The chart tracks the Features completed each Sprint by all the teams in an ART.

Tracking Progress on the PI Objectives

PI Objectives are intended as a guiding and focusing aid for Product Owners during the PI. Tracking progress towards your objectives is essential for staying motivated, celebrating your wins, and making adjustments when needed. In an earlier chapter, we saw how to properly define the PI Objectives.

Unfortunately, too often Agile Teams define the objectives at PI Planning, and then forget about them focusing entirely on the tactical work of developing the Stories in their backlog. At the end of the PI, they assess the objectives achieved and move on. PI Objectives become "just another thing" that we need to do.

When managed properly and tracked throughout the Sprints, objectives can be a powerful tool to help Product Owners keep the focus of the work, maintain alignment, and give a sense of purpose to their teams.

A useful technique to track the objectives and to create transparency is to use a table like this:

Objective	Target end state	Target delivery date	On-track / Off-track / At-risk	% Delivered

Objective: This is the Objective we have defined for the PI. Remember that objectives are specified in terms of outcomes we want to deliver (and not in terms of outputs). This could be your Product Goal, or the "O" part of an OKR.

Target end state: Having an objective without a clear end state is not really actionable. We need to be clear which end state we want to achieve, so that we can measure if we have done that. If using OKR, this is the "KR" part. If using SMART objectives, they need to be Specific and Measurable. Basically, we should be able to answer the questions:

"How do we know if we have achieved the objective?"

"What end state should we see?"

Target delivery date: Objectives should be time-bound, so we need to be clear about what is the timeframe. For PI Objectives, this could be the end of a specific Sprint by which you intend to deliver the objective, or the of the overall PI.

On-track / Off-track / At-risk: This column provides an indication about progress on each objective. It allows the Agile Team to make a quick assessment of the status of each objective.

% Delivered: This column helps the Product Owner identify how much of each objective has been delivered so far. When the number is below 100%, it provides a signal to the Product Owner that an objective may require additional focus from the team, or may be at risk.

This table is a useful tool for Product Owners to update throughout the Sprints to track progress. In fact, Product Owners should:

- Update this table at least once per Sprint.

- Sync up and align with the team members to know what the status of the work is on each objective.

- Share the table with stakeholders at Sprint Review or System Demo, to create transparency and to set expectations for what will be delivered.

- Highlight those objectives that are Off-track or At-risk so that team members can discuss ways to adjust their work (e.g., they could do this at Daily Scrum or at Sprint Planning).

- Order the objectives in this table based on the Business Value of each objective (those with higher value should be listed first as we want to focus on them).

- Sync up with Product Management to align team objectives with overall ART objectives.

Product Managers can use a similar approach to track objectives at the ART level. A good time to review and to share the status of the objectives is at the PO Sync, when Product Managers and Product Owners meet to discuss progress of the work and to decide what to do next.

Business Value for PI Objectives

Assigning Business Value to the PI Objectives

Typically, PI Objectives are identified on day 1 of PI Planning, and further refined on day 2. By the end of the second day, each team should have a pretty solid list of objectives for the PI.

The Business Owners (these could be the key stakeholders for the product, or the executives in the company) visit each team's space and review the PI Objectives. Then, they assign business value[xli] to each of these objectives.

"What is business value?"

It is a score that the Business Owners assign to each objective, based on the value that they think that objective will deliver to the business or to the customers. The score tries to answer the question:

"How valuable would it be to actually deliver that objective?"

The business value is assigned with a score of 1 to 10, with 10 being the most valuable.

Business value defined for PI Objectives

Example for an Uber-like app.

PI Objectives

	BV
Save credit card in the app for future payments to avoid re-entering the card data again	9
Reduce customer's anxiety by proving real-time location of the car on a map while riding, so they know where it's going	10
Share updates on my location in real time with other people (friends, family) at least every minute	8
Allow user to select a specific car model or driver even if it means waiting longer for a ride	5
Redesign the User Interface to make it more user-friendly and reduce learning time to less than 2 minutes	7

Uncommitted objectives

	BV
Allow a car to pick up multiple users at different locations on the same path to save gas and provide cheaper rates	5
Enable monthly subscriptions for users who ride often and want a predictable cost of transportation	5

	BV
Total	39

Total Business Value is calculated only for committed objectives

This is a fictional example, for illustrative purposes.
Uber is a registered trademark of Uber Technologies, Inc.

The interesting thing at this point is that the Business Owners assign a business value to every PI Objective, whether committed or uncommitted by the team. They assign a business value to the uncommitted objectives too, because these are things that the team is going to do, even if the team feels unsure.

Then the team calculates the **total business value**. This adds up the business values <u>only for the committed objectives</u>, not for the uncommitted.

Example of Business Value

The calculations of business value are often tricky for people to grasp. They are based on simple concepts, but the mechanics may seem confusing at first. To get some practice with the calculations, and develop more confidence, let us look at an example.

Imagine that you are the Business Owner of a new startup that is building an Uber-like app, which is a new competitor. The team has identified a list of objectives that it would like to deliver in the next PI. You are going to assign business value to each of these objectives, for example, to understand which one is the most valuable objective.

There is an example in the picture. The total business value is calculated only for committed objectives. If you add up all the **business values**, you get a <u>total number of 39</u>, and this includes every committed objective. So, in this case, we have 39 points of value that the team plans to deliver by the end of the PI (notice that the uncommitted objectives are not included in the count).

Knowing the value that the business assigns to a team's objectives provides additional context for decisions on priorities during the PI. For example, if a team is struggling to complete all of the work, and it needs to decide what to prioritize, it can consider the business value of different objectives and prioritize the one with the highest value.

Evaluating Actual Business Value Delivered at the End of the PI

Let us jump to the future by a few weeks, to see what happens at the business value at the end of the PI. The Business Owners again are going to review each of the PI Objectives, and they are going to score each objective on the actual business value delivered. They assign a new score to each objective called the actual business value. Based on the work that the team has actually completed, the score represents the value that the team has delivered on each of the objectives.

Actual business value and team's effectiveness measure

Example for an Uber-like app.

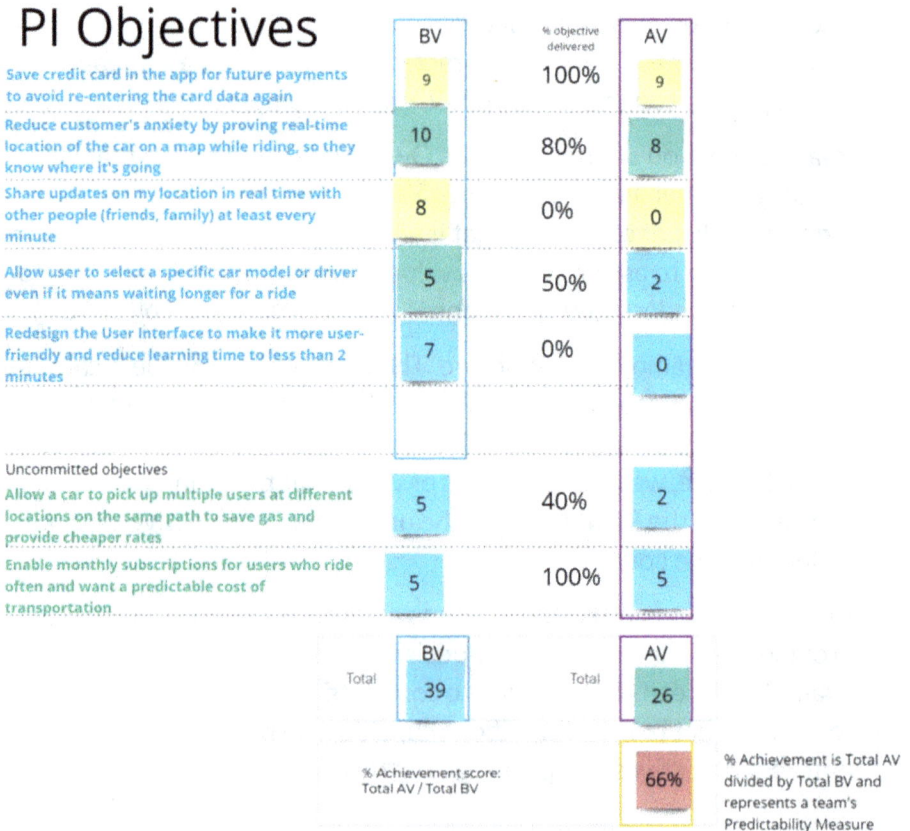

PI Objectives

PI Objectives	BV	% objective delivered	AV
Save credit card in the app for future payments to avoid re-entering the card data again	9	100%	9
Reduce customer's anxiety by proving real-time location of the car on a map while riding, so they know where it's going	10	80%	8
Share updates on my location in real time with other people (friends, family) at least every minute	8	0%	0
Allow user to select a specific car model or driver even if it means waiting longer for a ride	5	50%	2
Redesign the User Interface to make it more user-friendly and reduce learning time to less than 2 minutes	7	0%	0
Uncommitted objectives			
Allow a car to pick up multiple users at different locations on the same path to save gas and provide cheaper rates	5	40%	2
Enable monthly subscriptions for users who ride often and want a predictable cost of transportation	5	100%	5

	BV		AV
Total	39	Total	26

% Achievement score:
Total AV / Total BV

66% — % Achievement is Total AV divided by Total BV and represents a team's Predictability Measure

This is a fictional example, for illustrative purposes.
Uber is a registered trademark of Uber Technologies, Inc.

Sometime, the team is able to deliver 100% of the objectives and therefore they deliver 100% of the business value. Sometimes, the team is not able to deliver 100% of the objectives, and the actual value delivered is lower than the initial business value.

The actual value is assigned to all of the objectives, whether committed or uncommitted, to account for all of the work delivered by the team in the PI.

The team can then calculate the total actual value, by adding up the scores assigned for actual value to each objective – in this case, <u>both the committed and the uncommitted</u>.

Example of Actual Value

In our example, the first objective was delivered 100% and the team got 9 points. The second objective was delivered 80%, so they got 8 points. For the third objective, the team struggled to even start it, and it delivered 0%, so 0 points.

And then if you go down the list, you get to those 2 objectives at the bottom. They were uncommitted; however, the team delivered 40% for one, and 100% for the other.

In our example, the team delivered 26 points of total actual value. Remember that at the beginning of the PI, the team had committed to a total business value of 39, and it delivered 26.

The Team's Achievement Score

We can divide the total actual value by the total business value. That determines the **team's achievement score**. That number measures planning predictability: how predictable is the team at planning and delivering its work. Ideally, we want that number to be around 100%. When you are in that range, it means that the team is pretty good at planning and at setting the right expectations. In practice, the achievement score may vary between 80% and 120%.

To continue with the prior example, the team achieved a score of 66% (26 divided by 39). It seems that the team overcommitted itself to too many objectives or to objectives that were too large to achieve in a single PI. Or the team may have faced unexpected impediments, or it had some dependencies that did not get resolved in time. Whatever the reasons, these can be prompts to start the conversation and to find suggestions for the team on how to improve.

The team's achievement score is a useful metric to identify how predictable the team is in delivering on its plans. Typically, a number that is too low indicates that the team is overcommitting in its plan or is committing to unreasonable objectives. When the achievement score is far from 100%, it signals an opportunity for retrospective and continuous improvement: there is probably something going on with the team, and it may be worth a conversation. Maybe the SM (Scrum Master) or the RTE (Release Train Engineer) can work with the team to see if they can help the team improve.

ART Predictability Measure

A similar calculation can be done at the ART level. The achievement score for each Agile Team can be rolled up to create the ART predictability measure. This shows how predictable the ART is at planning and delivering on the PI Objectives. Any variations outside of the 80-120% range should be interpreted as an opportunity for improvement.

Improving Flow Through Your System

SAFe is a flow-based framework: it is heavily influenced by Lean concepts, and maximizing flow is a key objective of Lean. In fact,

> *"Any interruptions to flow must be identified and addressed systematically to enable continuous value delivery."*

Scaled Agile, Inc.

The goal of SAFe is to deliver a continuous flow of value to the customers and to the business. To sustain flow, teams need to continually measure flow metrics and to identify bottlenecks for continuous improvement.

Several situations can limit the flow of value in an Agile or SAFe team, hindering their ability to deliver working software frequently and efficiently. For example:

Process and workflow issues

- **Excessive Work in Process (WIP):** Working on too many tasks at once or continuously changing priorities lead to context switching, delays, and decreased focus. Implement WIP limits to streamline flow and to minimize bottlenecks.

- **Dependencies and handoffs:** Dependencies between team members or across teams create delays and communication breakdowns. Leverage the ART Planning Board appropriately to foster shared ownership and to promote cross-functional collaboration.

- **Big upfront planning:** Planning the work on entire Epics or Features without rapid validation of the ideas before committing to the full build, leads to wasted efforts, unused Features, and bloated products. Instill a culture of rapid validation and iterative development. Use MVPs or MVFs to test key hypotheses before committing to a full build.

Technical challenges

- **Technical debt:** Accumulated technical problems like poor code quality or outdated infrastructure create hidden costs and impede progress. Invest in technical remediation and refactoring.

- **Limited testing capacity:** Inadequate testing capabilities can lead to undetected bugs and an increase in technical debt. Optimize testing practices and utilize test automation to increase coverage and speed.

- **Lack of DevOps practices:** DevOps practices support technical excellence, increase quality, and improve the speed of development.

People and communication issues

- **Lack of clear product vision and priorities:** Unclear product goals and inconsistent priorities lead to misalignment and to wasted effort. Ensure that the team understands the vision and has well-defined priorities.

- **Poor communication and collaboration:** Information silos and communication breakdowns between team members or stakeholders can hinder progress. Foster open communication, utilize common platforms, and hold regular meetings.

The specific challenges will vary depending on your team and your context. Identifying these limitations and actively working to address them is crucial for optimizing flow and for delivering value consistently.

In SAFe, flow is supported at every level, through the adoption of Lean practices, technical practices like DevOps, and visualization of work with Kanban boards. Some examples of Lean practices that help teams improve flow include: Limit WIP, identify bottlenecks, minimize handoffs and dependencies, optimize batch sizes, reduce queue lengths, and visualize work in progress. SAFe offers ample documentation on managing flow on its website, and I invite you to read the relevant articles for more information[xlii].

Succeeding with SAFe

Adopting and Adapting SAFe

SAFe is the Scaled Agile Framework. It is widely adopted to help an organization to scale its Agile implementation. The power of SAFe lies in its breadth: an organization can readily adopt it to begin scaling. However, this strength can easily be interpreted as a weakness when the framework is applied rigidly or dogmatically, without consideration for the specific conditions or for the work environment.

Most of the companies I work with have either adopted Agile and SAFe practices or are in the process of doing so. They realize that adopting an agile mindset throughout the organization is key to becoming more competitive in the marketplace and faster at responding to changing customer demands.

Like any framework, SAFe is designed to adapt. Practices and tools should be adapted, expanded, and adjusted to fit the specific needs of the organization and its maturity level with Agile.

Becoming Agile versus Doing Agile

Applying the SAFe framework to an organization and "doing" the SAFe practices may be a good way to get started, but if the mindset and culture of the organization don't change, the teams risk just "doing" Agile, and not "becoming" Agile. To reap the benefits of SAFe, align itself with the market changes, and better satisfy its customers' needs, an organization should infuse a culture of agility throughout its ranks.

Business leaders should adopt the key principles and accept the iterative development model offered by SAFe to reduce risk, optimize return, and satisfy customer needs. Stakeholders need to feel comfortable with a (relatively) lack of long-term plans, and instead accept that roadmaps are designed to provide a short-term view and may change dramatically over time. Business leaders should appreciate the value of launching an MVP (Minimum Viable Product) in the marketplace as early as possible, learning from their customers, validating (or invalidate) hypotheses, and improving from it.

Often, executives struggle with adopting SAFe because the world they live in is nothing but agile. Quarterly forecast, Wall Street analysts, and shareholders, all expect clear plans and metrics that are met. Customers and partners expect a roadmap that extends well into the future. Agile is perceived as the antithesis of planning and is therefore resisted.

But at its core Agile methodologies are designed to control risk. Isn't this one of the most important tenets of any business?

Product Managers can help their organization become more agile by acting as champions and implementing techniques that enable executives become more comfortable. A key driver of agility is product thinking and Product Managers can promote this mindset by promoting the adoption of product practices as discussed in this book.

Start Small, Implement SAFe Incrementally

Several years ago, I was a Director of Product Development at Capital One (the *"What's in your wallet?"* bank, a top-10 financial institution in the United States) and I was managing a team of Product Owners who were building digital tools for our bankers and for our customers. We were at the beginning of a large Agile transformation, and I had the opportunity to experiment with different practices.

I remember one day my boss wanted me to learn more about this *"new thing called SAFe"* – he had heard about it at the annual Agile conference, and suggested that I find out if it can benefit my teams. I went online and learned about the Agile Release Train, about PI Planning, and about using a Portfolio Backlog to prioritize Epics.

Without hesitation, I suggested to my product team that we practice some of the SAFe concepts. We started organizing our work in quarterly increments. At the beginning of each quarter, we did a short PI Planning by prioritizing an Epics backlog using WSJF (Weighted Shortest Job First) and by selecting the key priorities for the upcoming quarter. My team would then break down the selected Epics into work items for each Team backlog and execute the work in Sprints. We repeated the process the following quarter by re-prioritizing the Epics backlog and by selecting the top 2-3 things to deliver next. That was a quick way for us to adopt some of the SAFe practices and begin learning from them.

It created a huge amount of alignment and transparency with our stakeholders. We were just scratching the surface of SAFe, but in hindsight, that experiment gave us the leverage to extend SAFe practices to other teams, and then to an ART.

That is the approach I I prefer to take when scaling Agile. Do not build gigantic structures with hundreds of people all at once. Instead, take a more "agile" approach by adopting some of the SAFe practices within an ART, then evaluate and decide how to move forward. Scaling Agile can be both incremental and iterative, and you can learn a lot about what your teams really need by doing it one step at a time.

Any Tips to Implement SAFe Effectively?

By Brian Schweickert

The main thing is to remember, and to remind your clients/customers, that SAFe is a framework. Therefore, be open to adjust it to fit your organization, and be OK if you don't use every piece of advice. Every 'transformation' that I have been involved with wasn't 100% by the books ... we made it make sense for the good of the client/customer.

What Are the Key Benefits You Have Observed from Adopting SAFe?

By Ajiri Ideh, RTE, SPC

In addition to all the benefits of adopting Agile, SAFe in particular brings a sense of belonging to everyone in the organization. To illustrate this further, I have been a coach with companies that have adopted Scrum/Kanban at the team level only. There was quite a bit of confusion with managers and other mid-level personnel as they were not certain how to interact with the team. However, this was a minor problem compared to the massive pushback from managers who felt their authority was being taken away because they could not see where they fit in "this new way of working", some even feared for their jobs.

However, on the SAFe implementations I have been on, there has been relatively less pushback, as everyone could identify where they fit in the big picture. Collaboration was better, and people took pride in the fact that they had a role to play, and were better able to adjust to decentralized decision making.

Scaling Agile versus Scaled Agile

The terms "scaling agile" and "scaled agile" are often used interchangeably, but there are some subtle differences between them. Here is a breakdown:

Scaling Agile

"Scaling" is a broader concept than "scaled": In a sense, scaling never ends. It is a continuous journey for the organization as it learns and experiments with scaling Agile practices.

Scaling Agile is not tied to any single framework or methodology. It refers to the overall approach of adapting and applying Agile principles and practices to larger organizations and to complex projects. It is about finding ways to maintain the core benefits of Agile (flexibility, adaptability, and customer focus) while dealing with increased scale and complexity.

The focus is on principles: Scaling emphasizes adhering to the core principles of the Agile Manifesto, such as iterative development, feedback loops, and continuous improvement.

Scaled Agile

"Scaled" indicates an accomplishment, something that has been achieved. It usually refers to using a defined framework or methodology for scaling Agile, such as SAFe, LeSS (Large-Scale Scrum), or DAD (Disciplined Agile Delivery). These frameworks provide specific recommendations for roles, artifacts, ceremonies, and other practices to adapt Agile to larger environments.

In a sense, a scaled Agile framework offers a structured and prescriptive approach compared to the broader concept of scaling Agile. A key benefit is that it provides detailed guidance on how to implement Agile practices at scale and promises a faster implementation.

Here is an analogy to help illustrate the difference:

- Think of **scaling** Agile as building a house. You have the freedom to choose different materials, architectural styles, and construction methods depending on your needs and on your preferences.

- **Scaled** Agile frameworks are like predesigned house plans. They provide a specific blueprint for building a house, with defined materials, layout, and construction steps. You can still make some modifications to the plan, but it gives you a starting point and structure. It's faster to adopt, but it's less flexible.

Ultimately, the structure, the practices, and the overall approach to scaling depends on your specific needs and context. SAFe offers a predefined, ready to plug-in framework that can be applied to an organization and help it to scale.

However, to succeed with SAFe, you may want to expand beyond the guidelines and structure of the scaled Agile framework and to adopt it in a **scaling** approach[xliii]:

- **Understand what works** for your own context and what allows you achieve your desired outcomes.
- **Continuously inspect and adapt** your approach.
- As you acquire more experience and want more flexibility, you may shift toward a more **principles-based approach.**

Two Limitations of SAFe

By Bernie Maloney, CST

My firm opinion is that Scaled Agile is intellectually sound, but fundamentally flawed.

It is intellectually sound because each of the research articles they offer are pretty good. When I've gone through and looked at them in detail, I haven't found problems with the individual articles.

However, it is fundamentally flawed in two very evident ways, and it propagates a flaw that's pretty prevalent in industry:

One, Scaled Agile presumes that you are already doing good Agile at a team level. That isn't the case with most clients. In fact, most are often doing really poor Agile at a team level and they haven't made any of the shifts that are necessary to really engage Agile and get the benefits.

Two, Scaled Agile talks about the need to change mindset, but it does nothing to _change_ mindset. In fact, it further propagates a mindset that is prevalent in industry: that of the organization being a mechanism. So many times, people, when they see the SAFe "big picture", they think "oh, this is where I fit". Which means they don't need organizational change, and that's one of the problems.

Below is a visual I use in my own classes to explain the mindset element and why it is important.

Any existing system, any organization, has an amount of inertia that resists change. Anytime you try and change a system of people the change follows that of a Satir curve[xliv]. In Bruce Tuckman's language, you go from "forming" and into "storming" and you have to get through that before you get to "norming". "Storming" is uncomfortable, and because humans like stability.

When faced with change humans have a strong impulse to return to the prior status quo. When you apply the tools, the processes, and the practices of Agile, those only have a certain amount of counterweight to the existing organizational system and mindset. And this is why when you introduce Agile in an organization, it's likely to regress because of this organizational system and mindset.

To get leverage, you'll have to engage bigger things like the values and principles of Agile. Even those aren't big enough to offset things. To really affect change, you'll have to go all the way out to mindset.

Now that you see it, you also recognize that mindset is not all that visible or directly observable. That makes mindset **very** squishy, particularly for organizations that are focused on plan and predict. That squishiness is uncomfortable. If an organizational mindset has been based in plan and predict, and they are really craving something to scale Agile, SAFe is an easy fix because it does not require a change to this mindset. They stay comfortable.

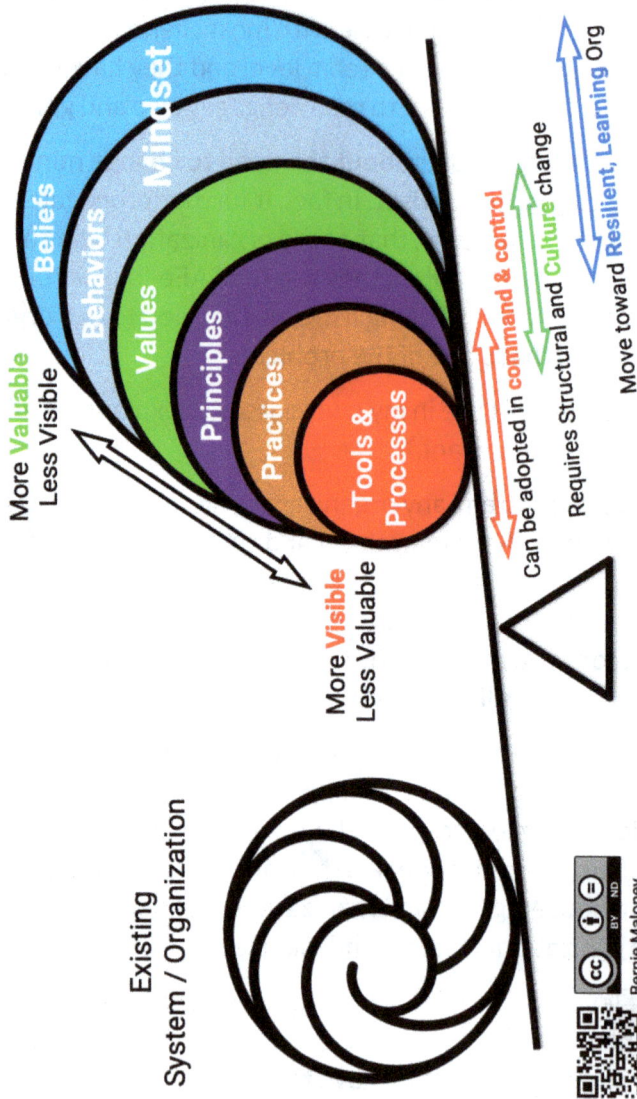

AGILE'S LEVERAGE = MINDSET

Mindset
Beliefs
Behaviors
Values
Principles
Practices
Tools & Processes

More **Valuable**
Less Visible

More **Visible**
Less Valuable

Existing
System / Organization

Can be adopted in **command & control**

Requires Structural and **Culture** change

Move toward **Resilient, Learning** Org

Image courtesy of Bernie Maloney

A big part of what I do in my practice is aimed to change an organization's mindset. My perspective is that getting an organization to scale really is about business agility. It's about shifting that mindset from thinking of the organizational system as a mechanism (the focus is on "what's our efficiency" or "what are the metrics that we have here?")

to thinking about the organizational system as an organism (one that can sense and respond to changing conditions and adapt to complexity).

Mechanisms you can plan and predict, but organisms sense and respond. That's a different mindset. SAFe propagates the mechanism model: big, complex, lots of moving parts. It propagates a "governance" mentality (consistent with mechanisms and waterfall and traditional project management).

Culture is where the resistance is to Agile. You have to change mindset to change culture.

De-scaling SAFe

Scaling agile to large organizations can become cumbersome and pose significant challenges. De-scaling, an emerging concept, advocates for a shift towards simplicity and smaller, more agile teams.

De-scaling tries to answer these questions:

"Do we need a large number of teams?"

"Do we need dedicated Product Owners and/or Scrum Masters for each team?"

"Do we need multiple hierarchical levels to drive decisions on the product?"

"Can we bring the planning and decision-making closer to the people building the product?"

There may not be a universal answer for each case – each situation and each organization are unique. However, exploring the answers to these questions may bring several benefits.

While SAFe offers a framework for scaling agile methodologies to large organizations, it might not be the optimal fit for every company, especially those struggling with organizational complexity, slow decision making, and command-and-control mindset. Adopting SAFe may exacerbate these issues rather than alleviating them. Sometimes, scaling agile with additional levels, new roles, multiple backlogs, and phase-gate approvals, can inadvertently cause a departure from the core principles of agility, such as rapid iteration and continuous improvement.

In the context of scaled agile frameworks like SAFe, de-scaling refers to the intentional simplification of the overall structure and processes to achieve greater agility and responsiveness. De-scaling promotes simpler structures and empowers smaller, more autonomous teams.

Benefits of De-scaling

De-scaling offers several compelling advantages for organizations seeking to increase responsiveness, foster innovation, and streamline operations:

Enhanced agility: De-scaling empowers teams with greater autonomy and decision-making power, enabling them to respond rapidly to changes and iterate faster. Smaller teams face less bureaucracy and can adapt to evolving market demands with greater agility.

Streamlined operations and reduced costs: De-scaling often leads to simpler organizational structures and streamlined processes, potentially resulting in reduced overhead costs and improved resource allocation.

Improved communication and collaboration: Smaller team structures foster closer collaboration and communication. This leads to better understanding, faster problem-solving, and increased alignment across teams and with stakeholders.

Enhanced employee morale: Empowering teams and fostering a culture of ownership can lead to higher employee engagement, greater job satisfaction, and improved morale.

Innovation: Smaller, empowered teams can experiment more readily and take calculated risks, fostering a culture of innovation and creativity. This can lead to the development of new solutions and quicker adaptation to changing market needs.

De-scaling in SAFe

While SAFe provides a structured approach to scaling agile, it's important to remember that it is not a one-size-fits-all solution. De-scaling principles can be applied within SAFe to achieve a more agile and efficient structure.

Focus on Value Streams: Instead of large ARTs (Agile Release Trains), consider smaller value streams with dedicated teams responsible for specific product or service areas. This fosters ownership and streamlines communication within the value stream.

Empower teams: Encourage self-organizing teams empowered to make decisions, manage their work, and set their own goals. Empower the Product Owner to make decisions on the product and own its outcomes. This fosters ownership, accountability, and a sense of purpose within the team.

Reduce ceremonies: Streamline or adapt SAFe ceremonies to be more efficient and relevant to smaller teams. Evaluate the necessity and duration of PI Planning and consider adapting it to shorter intervals. Consider if an IP Sprint is needed when teams are empowered to drive innovation via other means. This minimizes unnecessary overhead and allows teams to focus on delivering value.

Focus on continuous improvement: Regularly evaluate the effectiveness of your scaling and de-scaling approaches and iterate based on learnings and feedback. Don't follow a rigid playbook and instead find the right balance and set of practices that work for your specific context. This ensures your approach continues to be effective and adapts to changing needs.

Streamline the roles as teams mature: As teams mature in their ability to execute work and implement Agile and SAFe practices, they don't need continuous support from Scrum Masters and RTEs. The Scrum Masters can move to other teams, to teams that may be more junior in their Agile journey and may need more support. This allows the organization to focus coaching and support activities where they are needed, and to save money by consolidating experienced roles.

De-scaling is not about abandoning SAFe or Agile practices but rather about finding the right balance between structure and flexibility for your organization's specific needs. De-scaling requires a cultural shift towards empowering teams and embracing a more agile mindset. It is not a universal solution and should be carefully considered based on the specific needs and context of your organization. There may not be a single, "correct" way to de-scale in SAFe, and the approach should be tailored to your organization's unique circumstances.

Examples

Spotify

Spotify faced difficulties with scaling their agile framework, encountering slow decision-making and a disconnect between teams and the overall product vision. It considered a de-scaling approach by breaking down large squads (teams) into smaller, cross-functional "tribes" with greater autonomy and ownership[xlv].

As a result, these smaller teams achieved improved communication, faster release cycles, increased innovation, and a stronger sense of ownership among team members.

Netflix

Netflix is another company that continuously experiments with and reinvents its approach to product development. Initially, it adopted a hierarchical structure with waterfall development methodologies.

It gradually transitioned to smaller, cross-functional teams working in an agile manner, empowering them to make decisions and own their work[xlvi]. By doing this, Netflix was able to achieve increased agility, faster innovation cycles, and a culture of experimentation that contributed to their success in streaming entertainment.

"We strive to develop good decision-making muscles across our company. We pride ourselves on how few, not how many, decisions our senior managers make. [...]

We believe Netflix is most effective and innovative when employees across the company make and own decisions. We also believe fewer management layers makes us more agile."

"Context not Control" – the Netflix culture – Netflix.com[xlvii]

Challenges and Complaints about SAFe

Despite its popularity (or maybe because of it), SAFe has attracted its share of criticism. If you ask Agile purists about their opinion on SAFe, you may hear them talk like SAFe is the devil.

If many of the largest organizations in the world have adopted SAFe there must be something good about it. However, as the saying goes, "all that glitters is not gold" and SAFe has its share of challenges.

Here are some common complaints Agilists raise:

Complexity:

- **Steep learning curve:** With its multiple roles, artifacts, and ceremonies, SAFe can be overwhelming and complex to learn, especially for newcomers to Agile.
- **Bureaucracy:** Critics argue that SAFe adds additional layers of bureaucracy and meetings, potentially contradicting the core Agile principles of simplicity and flexibility.

- **Over-prescriptive:** SAFe offers detailed guidance, which some find too rigid and restrictive, hindering the organic adaptation that Agile encourages.

Scalability:

- **Poor fit for smaller teams:** While designed for larger organizations, SAFe might be overkill for smaller teams, adding unnecessary overhead and complexity.

- **Difficult to adapt:** Adapting SAFe to specific contexts and needs can be challenging, with the framework's specific components not always easily modularized or adjusted.

- **Focus on structure over outcomes:** Following the SAFe framework blindly, may emphasize adherence to its structure and to its rituals over delivering actual value and meeting customer needs.

Cost and Tools:

- **Training and certification costs:** Training individuals and teams on SAFe and on its certifications can be expensive, adding to the overall implementation cost.

- **Misusing tools:** Critics argue that relying heavily on dedicated tools for SAFe can lead to violating the first Agile value, "individuals and interactions over processes and tools," focusing on technology instead of truly understanding and applying Agile principles.

Misapplication of the framework:

- **Treating SAFe as a rigid process:** SAFe is meant to be adaptable, not prescriptive. Companies need to customize it to fit their specific needs and contexts.

- **Focus on compliance over value:** Following SAFe rituals without understanding their purpose can become an empty exercise. The goal should be to deliver value, not just tick boxes.

- **Neglecting cultural change:** Successfully scaling Agile requires a shift in organizational culture toward collaboration, transparency, and continuous improvement. Companies need to actively invest in changing mindsets and behaviors.

Often, these challenges stem from following the framework by the books, rather than by adapting to the specific context of the organization. Let us look at some examples of challenges and how to address them.

Complaint: SAFe Supports Top-down Decision-making

A reason why SAFe has been widely adopted, lays in its applicability to a traditionally hierarchical organization: the company needs to change very little about its structure in order to scale with SAFe.

While this is a benefit, it comes with consequences.

When the decision-making lies at the top, roadmaps, priorities, and requirements flow from the top to the people doing the work. This is how hierarchical organizations work.

Yet, in an Agile organization, we want the people closer to the work, and to the customer, to make decisions on the product. This ensures the delivery of value, increases speed to market, and reduces the amount of stuff built that no one cares about.

These two approaches seem to be in contradiction for an Agile organization. Yet, when done properly, SAFe can support both. You need to create an environment where Product Management and Product Owners collaborate and work together at defining solutions, validating them, and then prioritizing the work to deliver the most value.

One example of this collaboration is managing technical debt.

In a top-down hierarchical approach, priorities define the next big shiny Features to build for the customers. These are defined by Product Management and passed on to the Product Owners for implementation. The teams are pushed to accelerate delivery, causing them to take shortcuts and to accumulate technical debt. With requests for new Features coming down continuously, the teams cannot address their architecture and technical debt keeps piling up.

"So, how to break this cycle, deliver new features, and still manage technical debt?"

When Product Owners are empowered to manage their backlog, they can properly schedule and prioritize work that addresses technical debt. They can do this while collaborating with Product Management on building new Features. The Product Owners know the capacity of their teams, and can properly schedule work for new Features together with technical debt. They can use capacity allocation to create space for different types of work.

In this scenario, the product gets built incrementally and its architecture is solidly maintained over time. The teams deliver good quality work, and the Product Owners deliver value to the customers.

The key is not to treat Product Owners as the receiving end of decisions made by Product Management, and instead empower them to own decisions on the product, and the backlog, aimed at maximizing the value delivered.

Complaint: PI (Planning Interval) Creates Big Batches of Work

The PI Planning event is a planning opportunity that enables teams to plan ahead the work for the next 4 to 6 Sprints. PI Planning offers many benefits, but it has its challenges. When taken at face value, PI Planning creates a large batch of work for all of the teams in an ART (Agile Release Train) – the batch being represented by the total work planned for the 4 to 6 Sprints in the PI.

This, Agilists says, reduces the ability of the teams to adapt and makes the work incremental, rather than iterative: everything is set upfront and the teams just need to work for 4 to 6 Sprints and to deliver on the plan. One of the Agile values states: "We value more responding to change than following a plan."

"Is having a plan a bad thing?"

For some organizations, having a plan that all of the teams on an ART follow, is a positive thing. It creates alignment and focus, and allows the teams to deal with dependencies in a structured approach. Teams can focus on the work they have planned for the PI, and are much less subjected to changes of priorities, lack of focus, and impromptu requests from product leaders and executives.

When things evolve rapidly and when the ART needs to be more responsive (e.g., changes in the marketplace, or to customer requirements), the ART can select a shorter PI (4 Sprints) to be more responsive. When things are quite predictable, the ART can select a longer PI (6 Sprints) to be more focused on the plan. In a sense, SAFe provides the flexibility to adapt.

"What can Product Owners do to adapt their plans when needed?"

Even within a planned PI, though, Product Owners should continually assess whether the priorities they have selected, and the PI Objectives they have set for the PI, are still valid. The work is executed in Sprints of 2 weeks, and potentially the Product Owners can reassess their plans every 2 weeks, when preparing for the next Sprint.

If events in the market change, if a new priority comes up that is critically important, or if one of the PI Objectives is no longer valuable, the Product Owners should reassess their plan and update it. Because this may happen in the middle of a PI, they need to sync with other POs, and with other teams, to align their plans, to identify any new dependency, and to establish new objectives.

Of course, because one of the pillars of agility is Transparency, if plans change, they should be communicated immediately to everyone.

The idea is that the POs, and the Agile Teams in general, should collaborate with each other during the PI and reassess their plans if needed at any time. And not just to wait for the next PI Planning to do that.

Complaint: Story Point Normalization Leads to Team Performance Comparison

SAFe suggest a method to baseline a team's estimation using the "8 points per Team Member" rule. When taken to the letter, this method leads to every team using a normalized baseline for their estimates. And because their estimates become comparable, then – so is assumed – the teams' Velocities should be comparable. Hence, teams get evaluated based on their Velocity.

When organizations get there, they are in big trouble. A team's performance is no longer based on the value of the work it delivers, but is evaluated on the quantity of work produced. Teams become feature factories. The pressure increases to produce more. And the organization loses focus on what really matters for its business and for its customers.

"So, how to do estimations properly, and how to interpret story points?"

Let us rewind this a bit.

The SAFe normalization technique is a suggested technique for when a team is new and does not have historical Velocity. It is designed to get the team started with planning a Sprint's capacity when there is no other data available. It should not become an ongoing practice.

After the first Sprint is completed, the team should forget about the normalization technique (and any relationship between story points and number of days in a Sprint). Instead, after the first Sprint, the team should base its planning solely on average Velocity.

Which means that the meaning of "1 point" may be adjusted and a new baseline may be created by the team. Estimates should consider the effort it took to complete similar items in the past. Over time, each team develops its own mental anchor for what 1 point means.

As a consequence, estimates and Velocity cannot be compared between different teams.

In fact, Velocity is just a measure of how much work a team has completed in a Sprint. It is meaningful only within a team and cannot be compared with other teams.

In addition, Velocity indicates how much work a team has completed in a Sprint, but does not say anything about the value of that work (to the business or to the customers). Hence, basing team performance evaluations on Velocity is wrong.

It is important to remember that these are just some of the concerns raised about SAFe. Like any framework, it is not a perfect fit for every organization or situation. Carefully evaluating its strengths and weaknesses in your specific context, is crucial before adopting it.

Ultimately, the success of SAFe depends on its implementation and on its adaptation to the specific needs of the organization. Focusing on core Agile principles, tailoring the framework to fit your context, and fostering a culture of continuous improvement, can help mitigate these concerns and unlock the potential benefits of scaling Agile with SAFe.

The Verdict on SAFe

We said earlier that the Agile Teams represent the beating heart of SAFe and that (most) Agile Teams use Scrum at the team level. Scrum is both an incremental and an iterative approach. Products are built incrementally, one Sprint at a time. Scrum does not expect a full plan upfront. Instead, it supports discovery and validation along the way.

A Scrum team may build a solution in one Sprint, test it with customers, and learn that something should be changed. The team pivots, updates its plan, and then runs another Sprint building a different solution. The team continues to iterate on its plan until it finds a solution that works for its customers.

This team is embracing agility. An initial plan for the solution was needed, but the team was able to quickly experiment with the initial idea and learn that other solutions were better for their customers. As a result, the plan is updated, the scope is changed, and a new solution is developed. This team is embracing an iterative process to validate solutions and an incremental process to build them one step at a time.

Adopting both approaches together allows a team to deliver functionality incrementally to the end-users while at the same time to experiment and to refine solutions. Scrum provides the flexibility of both approaches. And since Scrum is at the core of SAFe, SAFe itself can be both incremental and iterative.

Unfortunately, the reality often is different, and it depends on the level of transformation your organization is willing to embark on.

Top-down Decisions Cause an Incremental Approach

If your organization is a hierarchical organization used to make product decisions, plans, and go/no-go decisions at the higher level, and the teams execute marching orders, the best you can achieve is an incremental approach. The plan is predetermined at the top, and the solution is given top-down. The teams are just required to implement it and they may do it one increment at a time until the whole solution is built.

Adopting Scrum at the team level and SAFe across the larger organization, may give you some benefits in terms of added transparency, higher collaboration between teams, and typically higher speed to market. The SAFe framework can be "plugged in" with minimum retraining on how the organization works, since the SAFe levels support a top-down approach, and an incremental development.

However, in this kind of organization, you are not going to see a transformation in the way in which products are ideated, validated, and built. You are not going to see an adoption of product thinking, a definitive increase in innovation, or a reduction in risk (the risk of building the wrong solution). Yes, you can put some customer-centricity or MVP (Minimum Value Product) lipstick on, but decisions are still made at the top. Teams build incrementally, aiming for a solution that is predefined.

Estimates suggest that 50%-80% of new features and product initiatives within established companies fail[xlviii]. These estimates vary by industry and by the type of products being built, and software development often involves more rapid iteration and experimentation compared to other industries. At such high rates of failure, organizations react with more controls and more top-down decision-making, reinforcing a product development approach based on big upfront planning and functional requirements being passed to teams for implementation.

Instead, to reduce the risk of failure, organizations should shift decision-making closer to the people doing the work (who also have deeper understanding of the problem and the customer needs). This is what empowered product teams do.

Organization Transformation Drives Agility

When you embark in an Agile transformation across the organization, it may require that you rethink the organization's structure and rethink how decisions are made. I am not advocating for lack of controls or for abdicating in favor of complete anarchy. Organizations need controls and need structures.

However, to reap the benefits of an Agile transformation, a few things need to change. For example, to adopt product thinking requires that Product Management and Product Owners work together and collaborate in the definition of the solution and its priorities. There are levels of responsibility still in place, but decisions are made together. This means empowerment, even at the team level, to be able to make decisions without all available information.

And empowerment requires context: Product Owners should not be relegated to executing priorities given by the higher levels, and instead they should be given access to customers, empowerment in finding the best solutions, and responsibility for solving a problem.

When you do that, you multiply the innovation engine of your organization 10x or 100x. Ideas and solutions are no longer limited to what the higher spheres can come up with (and let us be honest; all humans are limited, as so are the top executives). Instead, tens or hundreds of brains work together to innovate, to find new solutions to the customer's problems, and to see things in a different perspective.

Work becomes no longer incremental, but iterative. Product Managers and Product Owners understand that an idea for a solution may be limited, biased, ill-conceived, or sometimes just wrong. And, instead of embarking on a long journey trying to build it, they use iterative development and MVPs to run experiments, to learn from their customers, and to decide which – of many possible ideas – is the one that works best for the customers.

Now, the solution development process is both incremental and iterative. Decisions are made in full transparency by everyone involved in the solution development process. Innovation can flourish, and risks can be reduced.

This is the power of scaling Agile with product thinking.

About the Author

Valerio Zanini, SPC, CST, CPIT

A SAFe, Scrum, and Product Management trainer, Valerio Zanini is passionate about helping teams adopt agile practices and create products that customers love. With two decades of product development experience in a variety of organizations including Capital One, Cisco, Goozex.com and others, he helps organizations build new products in the early stages of product innovation, where uncertainty and lack of a clear solution are the biggest challenges.

He works with organizations worldwide to spark a culture of innovation and drive agile transformation. He is a Certified Scrum Trainer (CST), a SAFe Program Consultant (SPC), and a Certified Product Innovation Trainer (CPIT).

He is the co-author of "*Sprint Your Way to Scrum*", published in 2021 and the author of "*Deliver Great Products That Customers Love*", published in 2018.

https://www.linkedin.com/in/vzanini

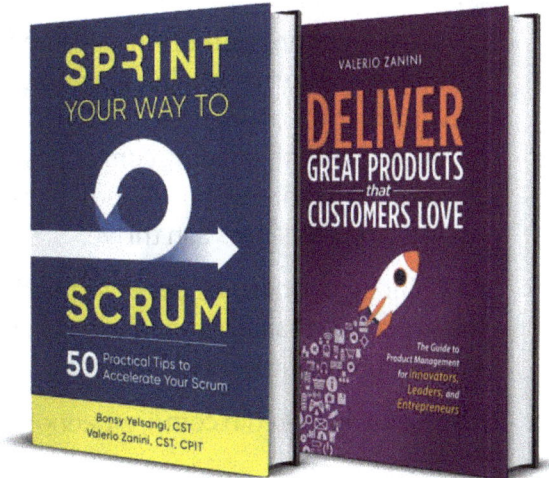

Expert Contributors

Luke Hohmann, SPC, SAFe Fellow

Luke is a four-time author, three-time founder, SAFe® Fellow, keynote speaker and internationally recognized expert in Agile Software Development. Coming from Silicon Valley, he knows how often founders focus on building companies to flip. Luke's passion is sustainably profitable businesses, because it is only through sustainable profits that a business can thrive.

As Chief Innovation Officer of Applied Frameworks, Luke works with the executive team to fulfill the mission of helping customers create sustainably profitable businesses.

https://www.linkedin.com/in/lukehohmann

Ajiri Ideh, RTE, SPC, MBA

Ajiri has over 18 years of experience working in the IT sector. She started her career in traditional IT roles (Project Manager, Business Analyst, etc.).

She got her first exposure to Agile in 2008, where she was a Scrum Master for a team piloting Scrum, within the organization she then worked for. She later spent over 7 years being a Product Owner and Product Manager.

She is currently an Agile Coach/Release Train Engineer (RTE), and the founder of Gold Consults Inc, a company that provides Agile transformation consultancy services and training.

https://www.linkedin.com/in/idehajiri

Anil Jaising, CST, Certified DevOps Trainer

Anil's career had an explosive start in the early 1990s, when he worked on a messaging product that sent messages across the world in 3 seconds, with a team that aligned with the Values and Principles of Agile. The product won the "Best Open Systems Award" in 1994. From the beginning of his career, he has been tinkering with code, infrastructure, product development and consulting in various industries.

His deep expertise in financial services and startups in developing business models have resulted in multiplying revenue and avoiding risk. He recently led a cloud transformation program for 250 application teams that saved one of the world's largest bank over $25 million. His deep Agile, DevOps, and leadership experience have guided multiple organizations achieve high throughput, market focus, productivity, and quality in building products. He has a deep interest in instructional design and is a certified Training from the BACK of the Room Trainer.

He is also a Certified Scrum Trainer with Scrum Alliance and a Certified DevOps Trainer with DevOps Institute. Anil is adjunct faculty teaching "transforming organizations" in the project management graduate program at New York University. He is well regarded in the industry as an Agile, Executive, and Technical Coach. He has helped several organizations successfully implement continuous integration, continuous testing, continuous delivery, and SRE practices. He is currently guiding the product marketing and development of a telemetry dashboard for Atlassian products.

https://www.linkedin.com/in/aniljaising

Vikas Kapila, SPCT, AKT, JMT

Vikas is an energetic individual with a proven track record of successfully facilitating highly complex transformations with significant business, technology, and commercial implications. These transformations involve multi-country, multi-discipline, and multi-cultural teams.

He is a seasoned transformation coach, adept at enabling the translation of business needs into achieved objectives focused. Vikas possesses a determined, innovative, and pioneering spirit, coupled with a considerate approach to risk-taking. With his results-driven attitude, proficient innovative business sense, and excellent technical expertise, he ensures a high standard of conversation and communication during the transformations he coaches. Vikas has honed excellent interpersonal skills through years of interaction in various countries and cultures. He excels at unlocking business value, simplifying the seemingly complex, and delighting customers within short timeframes. Vikas achieves these results by consistently fostering radically prolific, high-performing environments during his facilitation, guided by the belief to look, listen, and learn.

He is a trusted partner, synergist, and change catalyst with a consultative communication style, proven to unify stakeholders to propel business forward and accelerate business strategies. The successes of multiple transformations he has facilitated highlight his ability to hold the complete picture in real-time, inspiring teamwork and encouraging participants to construct, communicate, and collaborate to achieve the vision.

Vikas's mission is to enable teams and organizations to achieve better results and thrive in the constantly evolving marketplace.

https://www.linkedin.com/in/vkapila

Bernie Maloney, CST

Bernie's career started with a flash and a bang. Literally. His first position was designing devices that protect telephone networks from lightning strikes. A few career pivots later, he had a flash of insight: it was possible to tap into latent potential in every person, in every team, in and every organization.

The teams he has worked with have grown businesses to beyond $1B, delivering products from consumer electronics to network infrastructure, to services & payments, at firms including TiVo, Cisco, Wells Fargo, and more. He teaches private and public workshops, including several on Agile Product Development and Agile Leadership at Stanford Continuing Studies.

As a Trainer, Speaker and Coach, Bernie helps clients achieve performance breakthroughs with their teams, with their organizations, and with themselves. Moreover, he believes that Accelerating Genius℠ is possible in every person and in every business, and leads both to outrageous effectiveness, and to a whole lot more fun.

https://www.linkedin.com/in/berniemaloney

John Mulligan, SPC

Most recently, John has been training SAFe classes. Previously he was a Senior Consultant at Applied Frameworks where he helped agile teams by coaching, training, and mentoring. He spent several years as an Agile Coach, Release Train Engineer, and Scrum Master at Anthem where he launched the first Agile Release Train during their agile transformation. Prior to joining Anthem, John led multiple agile transformations at Capital One in numerous roles.

A graduate of the University of Southern California, the Naval Postgraduate School, and the University of Richmond, John is also a former nuclear submarine officer in the US Navy.

https://www.linkedin.com/in/johnmulligan

Ramesh Nori, SPCT

Ramesh Nori is a SAFe SPCT - SAFe Practice Consultant Trainer - for Lean Enterprises, a T-shape skilled professional in the world of Scaled Agile. His primary experience is in Executive consulting, coaching, and Agile advisory services coupled with Enterprise and Program/Portfolio transformation services.

Ramesh Nori is a Certified Lean-Agile Enterprise Coach (OMEC) as well with primary focus on Leadership team coaching and consulting.

https://www.linkedin.com/in/rnori

Thomas Nowaczyk, VP Product Management

Thomas Nowaczyk is a Vice President of Product Management at TransUnion, where he spearheads the development of identity data products aimed at streamlining customer experience applications. With a rich background in product management, Thomas previously served as the head of Risk Product Management at Neustar, which was later acquired by TransUnion in 2021.

Before his tenure at Neustar, Thomas made significant contributions to various organizations, including Rosetta Stone, Black and Decker, and began his career at JPMorgan.

Thomas holds an MBA from the University of Maryland and a B.S. in Finance from the University of Delaware. Currently based in San Diego, CA, he is deeply passionate about craft coffee, skiing, and leveraging identity data to drive innovation.

https://www.linkedin.com/in/thomas-nowaczyk

Brian Schweickert, SPC

With over 30 years of professional experience, Brian is a highly skilled SAFe/Agile Trainer and Enterprise Transformation Coach. He has assisted numerous enterprises through their transformation toward continuously delivery of high-quality releases that achieve superior customer value. As an instructor, Brian looks to bring in real world examples to support SAFe concepts that allow student to connect the dots between theoretical and practical.

https://www.linkedin.com/in/brianschweickert-agilecoach-spc

Jason Tanner, CST

As CEO of Applied Frameworks, Jason's passion is helping individuals and businesses discover software development practices that enable them to achieve better results. Profit = sustainability, and every business is capable of implementing profitable, sustainable software solutions.

Over 18 years of progressive leadership and management experience in enterprise software, IT, and the military helped Jason develop a breakthrough profit framework that revolutionizes the way you think about planning for profit.

https://www.linkedin.com/in/jasontanner

Bonsy Yelsangi, CST

Bonsy is a Certified Scrum Trainer (CST) and an Agile Coach. She is also the co-author of the book "Sprint Your Way to Scrum".

Bonsy has worked in a variety of industries, including media, remote managed services, luxury real estate, aviation, automotive, and private wealth management. Her IT background includes roles as QA Manager, Scrum Master, and Agile Coach for Waterfall and Agile teams.

She is the founder and CEO of Attain Agility, an organization that helps create an environment for teams that will help them – you guessed it – Attain Agility!

She educates people at all levels of the organization, from executives and leaders, to developers, PMs, BAs, and others working on project delivery. As a Scrum Trainer, she is known for her engaging style of training in person, as well as in the virtual world.

https://www.linkedin.com/in/bonsy-yelsangi-b86317102

Yuval Yeret, SPCT, SAFe Fellow, PST

As an agility coach/consultant/trainer, Yuval helps leaders pursue real and pragmatic agility at scale[xlix]. Leaders reach out to him when looking for ways in which to improve product development as well as when they want to apply agile ideas toward overall operational excellence and business scaling/improvement.

The engagements he thrives in involve taking an agile, pragmatic path to an agile organization. He is based in Boston and his clients are all over.

https://www.linkedin.com/in/yuvalyeret

Thank You and Acknowledgments

I want to thank all the people that helped me put this book together. The saying goes "... it takes a village..." and it cannot be truer than when writing a book.

In particular, I am thankful for the contributions of all the **Expert Contributors** with their stories and tips, all of which make this book richer and more interesting to read.

I am also thankful for the help and support offered by **Vikas Kapila**, SPCT, who read an early draft of the book and offered valuable insights about SAFe terminology, missing topics, and alignment to business agility; **Ramesh Nori**, SPCT, who read the book and provided feedback for improvement; **Andrew Sales**, Chief Methodologist, SAFe Fellow and SPCT, for his support and for writing a compelling introduction to this book; **Luke Hohmann**, SAFe Fellow, who continuously supports my endeavors; **Teresa Vickers**, RTE, who – unknowingly - gave me the spark to start this book when she asked me to train several Product Owners in her organization; the **legal team at Scaled Agile** for reviewing this book and providing guidance for approval; **Marilyn Silverman**, who is my tireless editor and has a keen eye for catching the inevitable grammar mistakes I make while writing; and my wife **Deborah**, who did not let me settle for an easier project and instead pushed me to expand my boundaries.

This book is so much better thanks to you all!

We Plant One Tree for Every Copy Sold

We are happy to work with ForestPlanet and their network of tree planting partners to implement our tree planting program. Please visit ForestPlanet.org to learn more about this amazing organization.

ForestPlanet

Footnotes and References

[i] The author compared publicly available adoption measures for SAFe, LeSS, DAD, and Scrum@Scale using a search on Google for adoption statistics of various scaled agile frameworks. As of February 2, 2024.

Framework	Estimated Adoption	Sources	Notes
Scaled Agile Framework (SAFe)	Over 20,000 companies	Scaled Agile website, various industry reports	Most popular framework, with various configurations and certifications available.
Large Scale Scrum (LeSS)	1,000+ companies	Less.works website, Agile Alliance Pulse Survey 2020	Simpler and lighter-weight than SAFe, emphasizes self-organizing teams.
Spotify Model	Internal use at Spotify and some larger organizations	Spotify blog, industry articles	More of a cultural shift than a rigid framework, focuses on autonomous teams and squads.
DAD (Disciplined Agile Delivery)	1,000+ companies	Disciplined Agile website, Industry reports	Flexible framework offering multiple configurations, promotes continuous improvement.
Scrum@Scale	Limited information on adoption	Scrum@Scale website, Industry reports	Less popular than other frameworks, focuses on scaling Scrum principles.

ii For detailed information on the Scaled Agile Framework, visit https://scaledagileframework.com/

iii https://scaledagile.com/what-is-safe/scaled-agile-benefits/ pulled February 2, 2024

iv If you are curious about learning more about SAFe, there is a lot of documentation online on a website called Scaled Agile Framework. I invite you to visit the website and to learn more about each component of the SAFe framework: www.scaledagileframework.com .

v https://scaledagileframework.com/product-management/

vi "The nature of product", Lenny's podcast https://www.youtube.com/watch?v=h-KVGHoQ_98

vii Scrum Guide: https://scrumguides.org/

viii "The Scrum Master is a Servant Leader" https://www.5dvision.com/post/the-scrum-master-is-a-servant-leader/

ix "The Scrum Master Competency Ladder" https://www.trulyscrum.com/scrum/scrum-master-competency-ladder/

x More information on this story, including videos and additional resources, can be found at: https://conceptsandbeyond.com/how-three-key-principles-transformed-a-banks-technology-landscape/

xi In Scrum, this is based on the Yesterday's Weather pattern, and typically we use average historical Velocity of the last 3 to 5 Sprints as an estimation for the maximum capacity in the upcoming Sprint.

xii At any point during a Sprint a Story may be in various "in progress" states depending on the particular workflow of the team. At the end of a Sprint, a story that is not 100% completed is "Not Done" and returns to the Product Backlog for further decision on next steps.

xiii The baseline thinking here is that each member of the team can do 1 point per day of work. This is a way to create a mental anchor for what 1 point of work is.

Because we have 8 working days in Sprint (removing Sprint Planning, Sprint Review, and Retrospective), we have 8 points available per person.

xiv The Lean Construction Institute (LCI) developed Big Room Planning as a way to coordinate and plan complex projects. The LCI was founded in 1997 by Glenn Ballard and Greg Howell. https://thinklithe.com/blog/big-room-planning-in-4-steps and https://leanconstruction.org/lean-topics/big-room/

xv SAFe website: https://scaledagileframework.com/pi-planning

xvi The Agile Manifesto, 2001: https://agilemanifesto.org/

xvii Scaled Agile provides guiding documents for RTEs on its SAFe Studio website: www.scaledagile.com

xviii Agile Metrics: 4 Balanced KPIs to Measure Success https://appliedframeworks.com/blog/agile-metrics-4-balanced-kpis-to-measure-success February 2024

xix "Product vs Feature Teams" by Marty Cagan: https://www.svpg.com/product-vs-feature-teams/

xx The distinction between clear, complicated, and complex works used here, comes from the Cynefin framework, created by Dave Snowden in 1999. Cynefin is based on the idea that different situations require different approaches. The framework itself is divided into four domains: Simple, Complicated, Complex, and Chaotic. By understanding which domain a situation falls into, you can then choose the most appropriate response.

Here is a breakdown of the four domains:

- Simple: Cause-and-effect relationships are clear, so you can rely on past experiences and best practices to make decisions.

- Complicated: Cause-and-effect relationships are not always obvious, but with some analysis, you can figure them out. Here, experts can be helpful in outlining possible solutions.

- Complex: Cause-and-effect relationships are unclear and emerge over time. In complex situations, experimentation and collaboration are key.

- Chaotic: There are no clear cause-and-effect relationships, and the situation is constantly changing. The best approach here is to take action to stabilize the situation and then reassess.

xxi "There is no Agility without Product Thinking": https://www.5dvision.com/post/there-is-no-agility-without-product-thinking/

xxii "Primed to Perform: How to Build the Highest Performing Cultures Through the Science of Total Motivation" by Neel Doshi.

xxiii Epic Hypothesis Statement: https://scaledagileframework.com/epic/

xxiv You can download that template from my website: https://www.5dvision.com/templates/epic-development-form/

xxv https://scaledagileframework.com/operational-value-streams/

xxvi You can download that template from my website: https://www.5dvision.com/templates/customer-journey-map-template/

xxvii For more information on Customer Journey Maps and a template to create them, visit: https://www.5dvision.com/templates/customer-journey-map-template/

xxviii Profit Stream ™ and Profit Streams ™ are trademarks of Applied Frameworks. Learn more at: https://profit-streams.com/.

xxix The Product Stream Canvas is copyright of Applied Frameworks, reproduced in this book upon permission from its authors. The book "*Software Profit Streams*" by Jason Tanner and Luke Hohmann is copyright of Applied Frameworks and can be found on Amazon at: https://www.amazon.com/Software-Profit-Streams-Sustainably-Profitable/dp/1544540671

xxx "*User Story Mapping: Discover the Whole Story, Build the Right Product*" by Jeff Patton

xxxi MVP Ideation Canvas: https://www.5dvision.com/templates/mvp-canvas/

xxxii I believe these activities are best done collaboratively between all of the Product Owners in an ART and the Product Manager(s). It may be important to include the Epic Owner too, or the person who defines and prioritizes the Epics (if different from the Product Manager). Some of the activities listed in this book should be performed by the entire product team together, to create alignment, to share context, and to empower everyone.

xxxiii *Radical Focus: Achieving Your Most Important Goals with Objectives and Key Results*, Christina Wodtke (2016)

xxxiv While the exact origin of the SMART acronym for objectives isn't entirely clear, it's generally attributed to George T. Doran. He first presented the concept in a 1981 article titled "There's a S.M.A.R.T. Way to Write Management's Goals and Objectives". It's important to note that the SMART acronym itself might have existed in different forms even before Doran's publication. Others like Arthur Miller and James Cunningham also contributed to the development of the SMART concept. However, Doran's work popularized the specific criteria that define SMART objectives, making him the widely recognized figure behind the acronym.

xxxv Irwin Mehr, Bob Atkinson Hedges, and Robert D. Irwin are considered the "fathers of risk management" for publishing a landmark book on business risk management in 1963, *Risk Management in the Business Enterprise*. The book covers various topics related to risk management, including the identification of risks, the assessment of risks, and the implementation of risk management strategies.

xxxvi Code of Hammurabi: This Babylonian law code (1792 BC) included provisions for compensating merchants for lost or damaged goods, demonstrating an early understanding of risk transfer. (Source: *The evolution of risk management* - Biblioteka Nauki)

xxxvii "Risk Management Techniques for Project Success" https://medium.com/@garypetercox/risk-management-techniques-for-project-success-38106e128b05 and "Control Implementation A Proactive Approach to Risk Mitigation" https://utilitiesone.com/control-implementation-a-proactive-approach-to-risk-mitigation - December 2023

xxxviii While the "Tiger, Paper Tiger, Elephant" metaphor seems widely used in risk management discussions, pinpointing a single origin or a reference is difficult as there are multiple origins for the terms. Anecdotally, references to "tigers" and to "elephants" in risk management appear as early as the 1980s and 1990s. However, these are isolated references without a clear connection to the specific "Tiger, Paper Tiger, Elephant" categorization as we see today.

xxxix The Risk Card can be downloaded: https://www.5dvision.com/templates/risk-card/

xl Unfortunately, pinpointing the exact inventor of the ROAM acronym for risk management is challenging due to its widespread use and lack of formal attribution. ROAM likely emerged organically within the risk management community, rather than having a single inventor.

xli The concept of "business value" for objectives isn't attributed to a single individual, but rather evolved over time through the contributions of several notable management thinkers and practitioners, such as: Peter Drucker (often considered the "father of modern management," Drucker emphasized the importance of businesses creating value for all stakeholders, not just shareholders) and Michael Porter (his concept of the "value chain" helped businesses identify and analyze the activities that create value for customers).

xlii ART Flow: https://scaledagileframework.com/art-flow/

xliii https://medium.com/@maxsermi/agile-at-scale-how-to-apply-agile-principles-to-large-organizations-45daca0a1432 and https://www.atlassian.com/agile/agile-at-scale

xliv The Satir curve, introduced by Virginia Satir, explains the evolution of an organization as it goes through change. https://www.knowledgetrain.co.uk/change-management/change-management-courses/change-management-models/satir-change-model

xlv Book: "Agile at Scale: Spotify and Leanpub from Startup to Enterprise" by Henrik Kniberg, Anders Ivarsson, and Par-Anders Fiorenius

xlvi Book: "No Rules Rules: Netflix and the Culture of Reinvention" by Reed Hastings and Erin Meyer

xlvii https://jobs.netflix.com/culture - March 5, 2024

xlviii Determining the exact percentage of new software product ideas that fail is challenging due to various factors:

Varying Definitions of "Failure": Defining "failure" in software can be subjective. Does it mean the product never launches, doesn't achieve user adoption, ceases operation shortly after launch, or fails to meet specific financial goals?

Limited Reliable Data: Many software projects aren't publicly disclosed, and internal data might not be readily available. Studies focusing specifically on software ideas are scarce.

Industry Heterogeneity: Success rates can vary greatly across different software categories (e.g., mobile apps, enterprise software, SaaS).

Nuances in Idea vs. Product: Distinguishing between a "new product idea" and a fully developed software product ready for launch can be difficult. Many ideas never progress beyond basic concepts.

Software development carries inherent risks: Estimates suggest that 50-80% of new features and product initiatives within established companies fail, and software development often involves more rapid iteration and experimentation compared to other industries.

[xlix] Yuval's blog: https://yuvalyeret.com/blog/exploring-the-controversy-around-safes-approach-to-product-ownership/ (reprinted with permission)